NATASHA JAMES

BREAKING

I0460125

THE
CODE TO
BUSINESS
SUCCESS

THE ULTIMATE GUIDE TO LUNCHING A SUCCESSFUL STARTUP: FROM IDEA TO GROWTH

Breaking the Code to Business Success

Copyright © 2025 by Natasha James.

All Rights Reserved

DEDICATION

This book is dedicated to all the dreamers—those who know deep in their hearts that they are destined for more. Remember, your dreams can never become a reality if you never start. Your life's circumstances will only limit you if you allow them to. Take that first step, and trust that you have everything you need to succeed.

ACKNOWLEDGMENTS

To my beautiful children—Earnest, Natyra, Kinsley, and Ian—thank you for being my greatest motivation and the reason I push forward every day. To my amazing husband of 23 years (35 years together), thank you for your unwavering support, patience, and love. You have been my rock through it all.

To my awesome goddaughter, Ladira James Richardson—thank you for your encouraging words, for motivating me to take on this task, and for pushing me across the finish line. Your belief in me means the world.

Lastly, to everyone who has been a part of my journey, believed in my vision, and cheered me on—I am forever grateful. This book wouldn't be possible without your support.

TABLE OF CONTENTS

INTRODUCTION

WHO THIS BOOK IS FOR

If you've ever felt like you're building a dream with nothing but grit and prayer, this is for you. I wrote this book for the woman who's tired of playing small, the mom juggling everything, the underdog trying to break generational curses, and the ambitious soul who knows she's meant for more.

If any of the following sound like you, then you're in the right place:
• You've got more vision than resources.
• You want to build something real but don't know where to start.
• You're balancing bills, babies, and a big dream.
• You're ready to stop surviving and start thriving.

Whether you're just sketching your first idea on a napkin or running a small business that needs clarity and direction, this book will meet you where you are—and help you take the next bold step.

This book is especially for:
• Aspiring entrepreneurs with a passion to start something new
• First-time business owners looking for guidance
• Professionals seeking a career change or side hustle
• Individuals with a business idea but unsure how to move forward
• Existing business owners looking to scale or improve their processes
• Students and recent graduates considering entrepreneurship

Who This Book May Not Be For

- Seasoned entrepreneurs looking for advanced growth strategies or complex business models might find this book too basic, as it focuses on foundational startup principles.
- Niche-specific businesses that require highly specialized knowledge might benefit more from industry-specific resources.

Finding Purpose in Your Journey

There's something powerful about embracing your own potential. I've seen women from all walks of life who were once afraid to take that first step toward entrepreneurship. They were overwhelmed, uncertain, and hesitant. However, what they all had in common was a burning desire to change their circumstances, to build something that not only supported them but also left a lasting legacy. This book is not just about creating a business; it's about breaking the cycle of doubt, hesitation, and fear.

I know what it's like to feel unqualified but chosen. To wonder whether you're enough. To feel like the odds are stacked against you. But I also know that greatness doesn't come from waiting for permission; it comes from stepping into your purpose, even when you feel unprepared.

Why Start a Business?

Owning a business gives you the power to shape your future. Whether you're looking for financial independence, creative freedom, or the ability to make a lasting impact, starting your own venture can change your life. My journey, from working multiple jobs to building businesses that positively impact my community, proves that anyone can do it. All you need is the willingness to learn, adapt, and keep moving forward despite the challenges.

STEPPING INTO ENTREPRENEURSHIP

I remember the moment I decided to take my first step toward entrepreneurship. I didn't have a perfect plan or endless resources. I was 20 with a baby and no blueprint. I didn't go straight to college. I worked jobs that paid the bills but didn't feed my spirit. Despite these, I became the first in my family to earn a degree, the first to buy a building, and the first to run multiple businesses. I did not have connections, wealth, or a roadmap. What I had was a belief that I was destined for more. I started small—selling services, building connections, and learning on the go. I figured it out—and you can too.

My first business wasn't about making millions; it was about proving to myself that I could do it.

Every milestone I hit was a reminder that the journey mattered as much as the destination. When challenges came—and they did—I reminded myself that every successful entrepreneur once stood where I stood: at the intersection of fear and faith.

This book is your roadmap to navigating those crossroads. You don't need everything figured out to begin; you just need the courage to start.

"Commit to the Lord whatever you do, and he will establish your plans." - Proverbs 16:3 (NIV)

REFLECTION PROMPT

What does stepping into your purpose look like for you right now?

_____

_____

_____

_____

_____

Write down one small, actionable step you can take this week to move closer to your business goals.

_____

_____

_____

_____

_____

_____

Mindset Check-In

Take a moment to reflect on your entrepreneurial journey. Are you holding back because of fear or uncertainty? Remind yourself that small steps lead to big changes.

Prayer

Dear God, thank You for giving me the courage to pursue my dreams. Help me to move forward with faith and determination, even when I feel unqualified or uncertain. Grant me wisdom and resilience as I embark on this journey of entrepreneurship. I trust that with you by my side, I am capable of achieving greatness. In Jesus' name, Amen.

Let's get started.

IDEATION

TURNING YOUR PASSION
INTO A BUSINESS

"Where there is no vision, the people perish."
- PROVERBS 29:18

Every successful business starts with a passion, but it's the vision that propels it forward. It's one thing to have an idea, but it's another to see that idea clearly enough to turn it into something real.

When I was in graduate school, I didn't set out to start a business. I was just a mom who wanted good pictures of my twins. I couldn't afford to take them to a professional studio, so I decided to take the photos myself. As I posted the pictures on Facebook, people started to take notice. They loved my photos and began asking if I could take pictures for them too. What began as a personal project to capture my kids' milestones turned into Natasha James Photography. I didn't know it then, but I was turning my passion into a business. Although it wasn't perfect, and I didn't have all the answers, I took that first step.

That's the power of a vision—seeing potential where others don't and having the courage to start. Passion ignites your idea, but vision turns it into a plan. When I opened Pinkolicious Birthday Party Spa for Girls, it wasn't just about celebrating birthdays. I wanted every little girl to feel like a princess. My daughter's upcoming birthday inspired me, but it was the vision of creating a unique experience that transformed that passion into a profitable business. It wasn't easy. My husband had doubts, and I had my own fears. But I knew that if I could make one little girl feel special, I could do it for many.

Lessons Learned from My First Steps

Looking back, one of the most important lessons I learned was to start with what I had. I didn't have expensive photography equipment or a dedicated studio when I launched Natasha James Photography. I made do with what I had, and my commitment to quality and creativity set me apart. The same was true when launching Pinkolicious. It wasn't about being perfect—it was about offering something unique and valuable. Often, we get stuck waiting for the perfect conditions to start, but perfection is the enemy of progress. Sometimes, you just have to jump in and learn as you go.

Embracing Challenges and Moving Forward

Starting a business comes with challenges, and fear is one of the biggest obstacles: the fear of failure, the fear of judgment, the fear of not being good enough. But I learned to see fear as a sign that I was moving beyond my comfort zone. Each new challenge was an opportunity to grow.

One thing I often reflect on is how fear almost kept me from moving Pinkolicious to a larger, upscale location. It felt like too big of a leap, but I couldn't ignore the vision I had for the business. It was a leap of faith, but taking that step made the business profitable and indirectly funded the opening of Allstar Community Care. I realized that fear is a natural part of the process. The key is to keep moving forward, even when doubt creeps in.

IDENTIFYING A PROFITABLE IDEA

The process of ideation—generating new ideas and finding the right one to pursue—requires a mix of creativity and strategic thinking. To find a profitable business idea, start by engaging in brainstorming techniques that will help you uncover opportunities in the market. A good idea often stems from combining passion with practicality and recognizing where gaps exist within your chosen industry. Taking a structured approach to ideation can significantly improve your chances of landing on an idea that is both innovative and viable.

One of the most effective techniques is **Mind Mapping**. Begin by writing down your passions or areas of interest at the center of a blank page. Next, branch out by considering related topics, skills, or experiences you have. From each branch, think about the problems that others might face in those areas. For instance, if your passion is event planning, consider the challenges people encounter when organizing parties, like coordinating vendors, managing budgets, or finding unique themes. Mind mapping helps you find connections you might not have noticed initially and allows you to organize your thoughts visually. As ideas start to take shape, group similar concepts together to identify potential themes or business models.

Another valuable tool is the **SWOT Analysis**. This technique helps you evaluate the Strengths, Weaknesses, Opportunities, and Threats associated with your idea. Start by listing your strengths: what skills or resources do you already possess that will support this idea? Next, consider the weaknesses—are there areas where you lack experience or expertise? Opportunities are external factors, like emerging market trends or unmet needs, while threats include competition and economic downturns. Conducting a SWOT analysis gives you a clearer picture of how well your idea might fare in the market. It also helps you anticipate potential challenges and proactively plan for them.

Additionally, practice **Reverse Engineering Competitors**. Take a close look at businesses that are already operating in your chosen niche. What are they offering, and how do they attract customers? More importantly, where do they fall short? Perhaps they don't offer personalized services, or their customer support lacks responsiveness. Identifying these gaps can help you position your own business as a superior alternative. By examining what works and what doesn't, you can craft a unique value proposition that sets you apart. Competitor research is crucial not only for identifying opportunities but also for avoiding pitfalls that others have encountered.

Aligning Passion with Market Demand

A successful business is not just about following your passion but also about aligning it with real demand in the marketplace. A profitable idea is born at the intersection of passion, skill, and market need. Passion alone does not guarantee success. You may love baking cupcakes, but if there is no demand in your area or too much competition, it might not be a sustainable business model. Therefore, it's essential to bridge the gap between what you love and what people actually want.

1. **Identify Your Passion:** Clarify what drives you. Your passion is the fuel that will sustain you through the challenges of running a business. Start by asking yourself questions like: What activities make me lose track of time? What problems do I naturally feel inclined to solve? Your passion should be something that you can remain committed to, even when faced with setbacks or long hours. This intrinsic motivation is crucial, as it keeps you moving forward when external factors become challenging.

2. **Find a Problem Worth Solving:** People don't pay for passion; they pay for solutions. It's essential to look for common pain points or inefficiencies in your area of interest. For instance, if your passion is fitness, think about the common struggles people face, such as staying consistent with workouts or finding the right diet plan. Once you identify a specific problem, brainstorm potential solutions that leverage your skills. The key is to ensure that the solution you offer is practical, effective, and truly addresses the issue at hand.

3. **Determine Market Size:** Assess the size of the market that might benefit from your solution. Use tools like Google Trends to gauge interest in your idea. You can also analyze social media discussions, conduct surveys, or use platforms like Statista to understand market trends. If your idea revolves around an emerging trend, gauge how long-lasting it might be. A growing market indicates potential for long-term success, while a declining one might suggest limited opportunities. Understanding the size and longevity of your market helps you make data-driven decisions about whether your idea is worth pursuing.

4. **Monetize:** Think about how to generate revenue from your idea, whether through products, services, or subscriptions. Consider various monetization methods that align with your business concept. If you're offering a product, consider selling directly through an online store or partnering with local retailers. For a service-based business, think about offering tiered packages to accommodate different client budgets. If your idea involves content creation or knowledge sharing, subscriptions or online courses might be viable revenue streams. Be strategic about pricing to ensure profitability while remaining competitive.

TESTING YOUR IDEA

Before fully committing to your business idea, it's crucial to test its viability. One way to do this is by creating a minimum viable product (MVP), which is a simplified version of your offering that addresses the core problem without all the extra features. For example, if your idea is to open a fitness studio, start by offering pop-up classes to see how many people attend and are willing to pay. Collect feedback and iterate based on responses. Testing your idea before full-scale implementation minimizes risk and helps you refine your concept.

Another method is to **Conduct Surveys and Gather Feedback**. Reach out to your target audience and ask for their opinions on your proposed idea. Social media polls, focus groups, and online questionnaires can provide valuable insights into customer interests and preferences. Be open to feedback, even if it means rethinking your approach. Sometimes, your initial concept may need adjustments to better fit market expectations.

Finally, build a **Proof of Concept (PoC)** to demonstrate your idea's practicality. Whether it's a prototype, a landing page, or a basic service offering, having something tangible helps potential investors or partners understand what you're aiming to achieve. A successful PoC shows that your idea is not only feasible but also appealing to the intended audience.

By aligning your passion with market demand, you lay the foundation for a profitable and sustainable business. The goal is not just to pursue what you love but to do so in a way that meets a genuine need. Combining creativity with practical strategies ensures that your idea not only excites you but also attracts customers willing to pay for what you offer.

REFLECTION PROMPTS

1. What are you passionate about, and how can you use it to serve others?

_____

_____

_____

_____

_____

2. How can you take one small step toward turning it into a business?

_____

_____

_____

_____

_____

3. What fears are holding you back from bringing your vision to life?

_____

_____

_____

_____

_____

_____

Mindset Check-In

"Am I allowing fear to keep me from turning my passion into a business? How can I shift my mindset to see challenges as opportunities?"

Prayer

Lord, thank You for giving me a vision and a passion to build something meaningful. Grant me the courage to take the first step, even when I feel unsure. Help me to see the potential in every opportunity and to act on it with faith. Amen.

CHAPTER

MARKET RESEARCH

UNDERSTANDING COMPETITORS AND CUSTOMERS

*"For which of you, intending to build a tower, does not sit down first
and count the cost, whether he has enough to finish it."*
- LUKE 14:28

arket research is the foundation of any successful business.
It involves analyzing both your competition and potential
customers to see if your business idea stands a chance in
the real world. This step requires both qualitative and quantitative
research techniques.

When I first started Pinkolicious Birthday Party Spa for Girls, I didn't
know much about market research. My idea was rooted in passion, but
I quickly realized that passion alone wasn't enough. I had to understand
what other similar businesses were doing, who their customers were,
and what gaps I could fill. I began by looking at other party venues in

the area—analyzing what made them successful and where they fell short. I noticed that while many offered birthday parties, none focused exclusively on creating a luxurious, spa-like experience for little girls. That was my gap.

COMPETITOR ANALYSIS

To effectively position your business, start by researching your direct competitors. Understanding your competitors is a critical step in crafting a successful business strategy. It's not just about knowing who they are but also understanding their strengths, weaknesses, and how they operate. Competitor analysis involves a thorough investigation of the market landscape, helping you identify opportunities to set your business apart.

Start by asking fundamental questions: Who are your main competitors? What products or services do they offer? Are they catering to a similar demographic as you, or are they targeting a different niche within the same industry? Understanding these aspects will give you a clearer picture of the competitive landscape. By identifying their core offerings, you can pinpoint what makes them successful and where they may be lacking.

One effective way to analyze competitors is by examining their **pricing models and customer base**. Pricing strategies can vary greatly within the same industry. Some businesses might position themselves as low-cost providers, while others focus on premium, high-value offerings. Determine where your competitors stand on this spectrum. Are they appealing to budget-conscious customers or those willing to pay more for higher quality or better service? Identifying these nuances helps you understand where your business can position itself. For example, if your competitors are charging premium prices, consider whether there is room for a more affordable option or a more specialized service that justifies a higher cost.

Next, focus on their **marketing strategies**. How do they reach their audience? Are they more active on social media, or do they rely heavily on local advertising and word-of-mouth? By analyzing their promotional techniques, you can assess what works and what doesn't in your industry. For instance, if a competitor has a strong Instagram presence but lacks a robust email marketing campaign, you might capitalize on that gap by building a strong email list. Additionally, observing how they communicate their brand message will help you identify whether your own branding is unique and compelling enough to stand out.

Another crucial aspect is to **look for areas where they may be falling short**. No competitor is perfect, and finding weaknesses can provide opportunities for your business. Are customers complaining about slow response times, poor customer service, or a lack of innovation? Online reviews, social media comments, and customer testimonials are invaluable for gathering this data. Once you identify these weaknesses, think about how to improve them within your business model. Perhaps your competitors offer a great product but lack a personal touch. This gap could be your opportunity to emphasize personalized customer service as a key selling point.

LEARNING FROM COMPETITORS

Sometimes, the most valuable insights come from businesses that are struggling or failing. When a local party venue in Baton Rouge closed down, I took the opportunity to learn why. It wasn't just a lack of customers; it was a lack of clear branding and consistent service quality. This taught me the importance of not just attracting customers but keeping them through consistent, memorable experiences. I made sure Pinkolicious had a distinct brand and a unique promise: to make every little girl feel like a princess.

By carefully analyzing why that business failed, I identified the key areas where my own business needed to excel. The closed venue did not create a unique identity, leaving potential customers confused about what they offered. I took the opposite approach by clearly defining what Pinkolicious was all about: delivering magical, princess-themed birthday parties that left a lasting impression. This clarity helped customers immediately understand what they were getting, which set us apart from others.

Moreover, the closed venue failed to build a strong, loyal customer base. I learned that even if you attract new customers, failing to provide a consistent and memorable experience will eventually hurt your business. As a result, I focused not only on attracting families to Pinkolicious but also on making each event so exceptional that they would want to return year after year. Repeat business became a cornerstone of my strategy.

Another lesson from analyzing the failed competitor was the importance of **consistency in service delivery**. Customers want reliability, especially when it comes to events as significant as children's birthdays. One negative experience can turn away not only the client but also their entire network. Therefore, I made it a point to train staff thoroughly, standardize party setups, and ensure that every detail—from decorations to customer interactions—was consistent across all events. This consistency reinforced the brand's promise and cultivated trust.

Learning from struggling businesses doesn't just mean avoiding their mistakes. It also means recognizing the areas where they initially succeeded. Sometimes, a failing business has a few aspects worth adopting, like a strong initial marketing push or a creative concept that was poorly executed. By extracting the good elements and discarding the problematic ones, you can develop a more resilient strategy.

ADAPTING AND GROWING

Competitor analysis should not be a one-time exercise. The market landscape changes, and businesses that were once thriving may struggle to keep up. Regularly revisiting your competitor research ensures that your business stays relevant. For example, if a new competitor emerges offering lower prices, consider how you can either match their rates or offer added value that justifies your pricing.

In addition, as you grow, remember that competitors may also evolve. A business that once seemed irrelevant might upgrade its services or rebrand to appeal to your audience. Keeping an eye on these shifts allows you to adjust your strategies proactively. Instead of being reactive, strive to anticipate changes by monitoring industry news, trends, and local business developments.

Competitor analysis is not just about finding flaws; it's about understanding the full spectrum of the market. By learning from both successes and failures, you position your business to not only compete but to thrive. Be proactive, observant, and willing to adapt your approach as needed. With consistent effort, your business can carve out a distinctive place in the market, building on the lessons learned from others while creating your unique path to success.

CUSTOMER ANALYSIS

Identifying your potential customers is a fundamental step in building a successful business. To effectively meet their needs, you must first understand who they are, what they value, and what motivates their purchasing decisions. Creating detailed customer personas helps you capture these insights, allowing you to tailor your product or service specifically to your target audience.

Start by asking yourself some essential questions:
- What pain points do your potential customers have?
- What motivates them to make a purchase?
- How can your solution fit seamlessly into their lives?

A customer persona is essentially a semi-fictional representation of your ideal customer based on data and research. It includes demographics (age, gender, income level), behaviors (shopping habits, brand preferences), and needs (what they are looking for in a product or service). By creating personas, you avoid the pitfall of trying to market to everyone, which often results in diluted efforts and less impactful marketing strategies.

One way to develop a customer persona is by collecting data through surveys, social media insights, and customer feedback. Look for patterns—do your most loyal customers share similar characteristics or challenges? Use this information to build a profile that represents a typical buyer, including their goals, challenges, and preferred communication channels.

For instance, when I started Pinkolicious Birthday Party Spa for Girls, I initially thought that any parent planning a birthday party was a potential customer. However, through trial and error, I discovered that my ideal customers were mothers who valued a high-quality, themed experience and were willing to invest in a memorable event for their daughters. These mothers were typically in their 30s to 40s, had a moderate to high household income, and often sought unique, boutique-style celebrations. Realizing this allowed me to focus my marketing efforts more effectively, targeting those who appreciated the special touches we offered rather than trying to appeal to everyone.

FINDING YOUR IDEAL CUSTOMER

One of the challenges I faced when starting Pinkolicious was the assumption that every parent who wanted a birthday party was a potential customer. I learned that not all parents were willing to pay a premium for themed parties. Some preferred simple, budget-friendly options, while others valued an immersive, princess-themed experience. It took time to understand that I couldn't be all things to all people. Trying to appeal to everyone led to mixed messages and inconsistent branding.

Once I identified that my ideal customers were mothers looking for a personalized, upscale experience, I adjusted my marketing accordingly. Instead of promoting generic birthday packages, I highlighted our unique features—custom spa treatments, personalized party themes, and elegant decor. I also focused on building relationships with local moms' groups and community influencers who valued these types of experiences.

MARKET TRENDS

Keeping an eye on industry trends is crucial for staying relevant and competitive. Market trends reveal the direction the industry is moving, highlighting new opportunities and potential challenges. One significant trend I noticed while running Pinkolicious was the increasing demand for social media-worthy experiences. Parents didn't just want a birthday party; they wanted an event that looked beautiful in photos and could be shared online. This insight led me to focus on creating aesthetically pleasing setups and Instagram-worthy moments within each party package.

Another trend that greatly impacted Pinkolicious was the rise of personalized experiences. Parents were no longer content with cookie-cutter party themes. They wanted something that reflected their child's personality and interests. To meet this demand, I offered customizable packages where parents could choose everything from the color scheme to the activities. This approach not only appealed to our target market but also differentiated us from competitors who offered generic party plans.

ADAPTING TO CHANGE

Adapting to market changes is essential for long-term success. During the COVID-19 pandemic, many businesses in the event planning industry faced significant challenges. Restrictions on gatherings meant fewer in-person parties, which directly impacted revenue. Instead of waiting for things to return to normal, I chose to innovate.

I introduced smaller, more personalized party packages tailored to immediate family gatherings and virtual celebration options that included themed party kits delivered to the customer's doorstep. These kits contained decorations, party favors, and step-by-step guides for creating a spa experience at home. This pivot not only kept the business running but also demonstrated our ability to adapt to shifting circumstances.

Adaptability became a key component of Pinkolicious' continued success. Being flexible allowed me to respond to customer needs even when traditional business models were disrupted. This approach reinforced the brand's commitment to creating special memories, regardless of external challenges.

TOOLS AND TECHNIQUES FOR TESTING AND VALIDATING IDEAS

Once you understand your market, it's time to put your business idea to the test. Several tools and techniques can help you determine whether there is enough demand to make your idea viable. Testing your concept early minimizes risk and helps refine your approach before making significant investments.

One effective method is conducting **Surveys** using platforms like Google Forms and SurveyMonkey. These tools allow you to gather feedback directly from your target audience. Craft your questions to gauge interest, willingness to pay, and preferences. For example, when developing new party packages, I surveyed local moms to understand what themes and features they valued most. The responses guided my decisions and helped me create offerings that resonated with potential customers.

Another practical approach is launching a **Minimum Viable Product (MVP)**. An MVP is a simplified version of your product or service that addresses the core problem without all the extra features. For Pinkolicious, the MVP was hosting small, themed parties at my home before investing in a dedicated space. This allowed me to test the concept and gather valuable feedback without significant upfront costs. Based on the positive responses, I moved forward with opening the full-party spa location.

Additionally, creating **Landing Pages** can gauge interest before a full launch. These pages briefly outline your idea and encourage visitors to sign up for more information. High sign-up rates indicate strong interest, while low engagement may signal the need to adjust your concept.

Testing and validating your ideas not only reduces financial risks but also provides insights into what potential customers truly value. This data-driven approach helps you refine your business model and align it more closely with market demands.

By thoroughly analyzing your customers, staying attuned to market trends, and proactively adapting to changes, you position your business for sustainable growth. Whether you are launching a new venture or evolving an existing one, understanding your ideal customer is the first step toward creating a successful, customer-centric business.

FEEDBACK LOOPS AND PIVOTING IF NEEDED

One of the most important aspects of running a successful business is the ability to adapt. After testing your idea, gathering feedback and being open to change is crucial. Sometimes, what you initially believe will resonate with customers turns out differently once your product or service is out in the real world. Listening to your audience and making necessary adjustments is a fundamental part of sustainable growth.

When I first launched Pinkolicious, I was convinced that parents would want long, elaborate birthday parties for their little girls. My vision included multi-hour spa experiences with detailed activities and extensive decorations. I believed that creating an immersive, all-day event would be the ultimate selling point. However, after hosting several parties, I began to notice a pattern in the feedback I received. While parents appreciated the attention to detail and the luxurious feel of the parties, many commented that the events felt too long for younger children.

At first, I was reluctant to make changes. I had invested a great deal of effort into crafting the ultimate princess experience, and I couldn't imagine scaling it down. Yet, the more I listened to my customers, the more I realized that their primary desire was to have a memorable yet manageable party. Parents wanted their children to feel special, but they didn't want to commit to a lengthy event that left both kids and adults feeling exhausted.

Instead of being discouraged, I took this feedback seriously and began to pivot. I introduced shorter, more affordable packages that still retained the high-quality elements Pinkolicious was known for. I offered a "Mini Spa Experience" that lasted just an hour and a half, featuring a few key pampering activities and a simple yet elegant setup. This new format not only aligned better with parents' expectations but also allowed me to host more parties in a single day, increasing profitability.

This willingness to pivot allowed Pinkolicious to thrive where others failed. By responding to customer feedback rather than stubbornly sticking to my original concept, I built a more flexible business model. My ability to adapt quickly gave me a competitive edge, as parents appreciated that I truly listened to their needs.

The Importance of Continuous Feedback

Gathering feedback shouldn't be a one-time effort. It's an ongoing process that keeps your business aligned with customer expectations. After implementing the shorter party packages, I continued to solicit feedback from clients. I asked them what they loved about the new format and whether there were any additional improvements they would like to see. This ongoing dialogue strengthened relationships and helped me stay ahead of evolving preferences.

I also learned that feedback doesn't just come from formal surveys or reviews. Sometimes, the most insightful feedback comes from casual conversations, social media interactions, or even observing how parents and children behave during the party. Being attentive to both direct and indirect feedback helped me understand subtle aspects that I might have missed otherwise.

Embracing Change and Building Resilience

Pivoting doesn't mean abandoning your original vision. Instead, it's about being flexible enough to refine your approach while maintaining your core values. When I decided to introduce the shorter parties, I kept the core elements that made Pinkolicious unique: the princess themes, the attention to detail, and the personal touches that made each event special. The format changed, but the heart of the business remained the same.

Being willing to pivot not only saved my business but also reinforced an important lesson: Adaptability is a strength, not a weakness. Entrepreneurs who cling too rigidly to their original ideas often struggle when the market shifts or when customers express different preferences. Embracing change is not about admitting failure; it's about demonstrating commitment to serving your audience in the best way possible.

Market Research as an Ongoing Process

Market research is not merely a one-time task; it's an ongoing process that helps you understand your competitors, customers, and the evolving market. By being diligent and open to feedback, you position your business for long-term success. Regularly reviewing what works and what doesn't ensures that your business remains relevant and continues to meet customer needs.

Staying adaptable also means being proactive about seeking feedback. Rather than waiting for problems to arise, I actively encouraged my customers to share their thoughts. I would send follow-up messages after parties, asking for honest opinions and suggestions for improvement. This open line of communication created a sense of trust and helped me continuously enhance the Pinkolicious experience.

TRANSITION TO LEGAL STRUCTURE AND COMPLIANCE

As I continued to understand my market and grow my business, I soon realized that having a solid business structure was just as important as knowing my customers. This realization led me to explore the legal foundations necessary to protect my growing ventures.

By keeping an open mind and viewing feedback as an opportunity rather than a criticism, I was able to evolve Pinkolicious into a more sustainable and customer-focused business. This mindset of adaptability proved invaluable when I expanded into other ventures, like Allstar Community Care. Drawing on my past experiences with Pinkolicious, I recognized that growth required not only a strong market presence but also a robust legal foundation. This awareness marked the beginning of my journey into understanding legal compliance and structuring my businesses to withstand challenges.

Through this experience, I developed a mindset that balanced creativity with practicality. I learned that being a successful entrepreneur is not just about having a vision but also about being willing to adjust that vision when necessary. Whether it's modifying a product, rethinking a marketing strategy, or changing the way services are delivered, the key is to stay resilient and responsive to the needs of your customers.

REFLECTION PROMPTS

1. Who are your top three competitors, and what sets you apart from them?

_____

_____

_____

_____

_____

2. What pain points do your potential customers have that your business can solve?

_____

_____

_____

_____

_____

3. How will you ensure your business idea remains relevant as the market evolves?

_____

_____

_____

_____

_____

Mindset Check-In

"Am I prepared to adjust my business idea based on feedback? How can I keep learning from my customers and competitors?"

Prayer

Lord, help me to approach my business journey with wisdom and a willingness to learn. Guide me as I research and understand the market, and give me the discernment to make necessary adjustments. Grant me clarity in identifying the needs of those I serve. Amen.

LEGAL STRUCTURE AND COMPLIANCE

"Let every person be subject to the governing authorities."
- ROMANS 13:1

As Pinkolicious Birthday Party Spa for Girls continued to grow, I realized that the more successful I became, the more I needed to understand how to protect myself legally. What started as a seasonal business that brought joy to children on weekends soon needed more structure and protection.

Pinkolicious was a relatively straightforward business. My primary focus was on creating memorable experiences for little girls. From tea parties to spa days, every event was centered around making each girl feel like a princess. Parents appreciated the detail and effort put into each party, and as word spread, the business continued to grow. However, it was a seasonal operation, primarily thriving during weekends and holidays when families were available to host parties.

Legal considerations back then were minimal—mainly liability waivers and basic safety precautions. At the time, I believed that was enough. My main focus was ensuring the parties went off without a hitch and that every little girl left with a smile on her face. I wanted to deliver joy and excitement without being bogged down by complex paperwork or legalities.

But when the opportunity came to open Allstar Community Care, a behavioral health agency, everything changed.

Entering the healthcare field meant stepping into a highly regulated environment where compliance with state and federal laws was non-negotiable. Unlike Pinkolicious, where the biggest concern was ensuring a fun and safe party atmosphere, Allstar required a structured approach to hiring, managing staff, and protecting client data. Liability protection wasn't just a good idea—it was a fundamental necessity.

In healthcare, the margin for error is incredibly slim. A mistake could mean a breach of client confidentiality, a violation of HIPAA regulations, or even jeopardizing someone's well-being. It wasn't just about providing quality care; it was about adhering to strict legal standards every step of the way. I had to transition from an event planner's mindset to that of a healthcare administrator, understanding that the stakes were much higher.

NAVIGATING THE LEGAL LANDSCAPE AS AN ENTREPRENEUR

One of the biggest lessons I learned from transitioning between these two businesses was that legal structures aren't one-size-fits-all. What worked for a party planning business was completely inadequate in the healthcare industry. Pinkolicious was about crafting joyful memories. Allstar demanded structure, regulation, and strong attention to legal detail.

At Allstar, I had to navigate complex regulations. The level of accountability skyrocketed, and compliance became non-negotiable. From handling client data protected by HIPAA regulations to maintaining licenses for mental health professionals, I found myself constantly navigating policies and standards to avoid potential legal issues. Every document had to be meticulously filed, and every process thoroughly documented. Compliance wasn't just about avoiding lawsuits—it was about building a foundation of trust with our clients and stakeholders.

The transition wasn't easy, but it was necessary. I had to accept that running a healthcare agency came with a level of responsibility that was far greater than anything I had experienced with Pinkolicious. By embracing the challenges and committing to learning every legal requirement, I ensured that Allstar Community Care would not only survive but thrive.

Building a Compliance-First Mindset

To build a compliance-first culture, I knew that my staff needed to see the value in these measures, not just view them as tedious tasks. It was essential to shift the mindset from seeing compliance as a burden to recognizing it as a fundamental part of our success. I realized that compliance could not be merely checked off a list. Instead, it had to be ingrained into our everyday operations and embraced as a core value.

We began by incorporating compliance discussions into regular staff meetings, making it clear that this wasn't just about avoiding penalties but about maintaining professionalism and trustworthiness. I wanted the team to understand that compliance wasn't an abstract concept but rather something that impacted how we served our clients and how we upheld our professional reputation. To make it relatable, I shared real-life scenarios where compliance made a difference, both positively and negatively. These stories helped the team see the practical implications and why it mattered.

One strategy that proved effective was setting small, attainable compliance goals and celebrating when they were met. For instance, after implementing a new data security protocol, I made a point to acknowledge the team's effort in adapting to the change. Celebrating these successes helped reinforce that compliance was not just about avoiding problems but also about building a stronger, more resilient organization.

Additionally, I recognized that my staff needed practical tools to support compliance, not just verbal reminders. We created checklists, easy-to-follow guidelines, and training modules that simplified complex legal requirements. By equipping the team with the right resources, they felt more empowered and less overwhelmed.

By making compliance part of our identity rather than just a requirement, it became less daunting and more manageable. The team started taking ownership of compliance practices, not because they were forced to but because they understood the importance of compliance and wanted to contribute to our collective success. Through this cultural shift, compliance became not just a duty but a shared commitment to excellence and integrity.

STRATEGIC PLANNING: BUILDING A COMPLIANCE CULTURE

I realized that legal compliance couldn't be a one-person job. It needed to be integrated into the fabric of our organizational culture. To achieve this, I had to shift from seeing compliance as solely my responsibility to making it a collective effort. Everyone, from administrative staff to clinicians, needed to take ownership of compliance practices. This realization was crucial because relying on one person to handle all compliance tasks not only created an overwhelming workload but also increased the risk of something being overlooked.

To make compliance a shared responsibility, I began implementing structured training programs. I held quarterly training sessions to ensure everyone remained informed and up-to-date on relevant regulations and internal policies. These training sessions were not just for administrative staff, who often handle documentation and data management, but also for clinicians who interact directly with clients and manage sensitive information. This holistic approach helped bridge the gap between administrative duties and client care practices, ensuring that everyone understood the bigger picture.

During these sessions, we discussed the importance of maintaining current licenses and certifications, which are critical in the healthcare field. One of the challenges I noticed early on was that staff members often assumed that keeping licenses updated was solely a personal responsibility. However, from an organizational standpoint, failing to verify credentials regularly could lead to compliance violations and potential legal issues. Therefore, I made it a standard procedure to check licenses as part of our compliance audit process.

In addition to discussing licensure, we focused heavily on following HIPAA protocols. Handling client data securely is not just an administrative task; it involves everyone who comes into contact with personal information. I made sure to explain the potential consequences of data breaches and the legal implications of mishandling protected health information. To make the training more engaging, we included real-world case studies where breaches had serious repercussions, helping staff understand why these measures are so vital.

Another key element of building a compliance culture was emphasizing the secure handling of client data. It was not enough to just implement protocols; we needed to foster a mindset where data protection became second nature. To achieve this, we developed practical guidelines on securing physical files, password management, and using electronic health record systems properly. Staff were given the opportunity to practice these protocols during training, which made them feel more confident and prepared.

By fostering open communication during these training sessions, I encouraged staff to share their own experiences or concerns about compliance. This dialogue helped us identify gaps in our current practices and allowed us to collaboratively develop better solutions. Instead of seeing compliance as a top-down mandate, staff began to view it as a collective responsibility.

Incorporating compliance into our organizational culture required consistent effort and intentional planning. By making it part of ongoing training and emphasizing its importance at every level, we successfully shifted the perception of compliance from being an administrative hassle to a fundamental component of professional practice. As a result, our team became more proactive in maintaining compliance, reducing the risk of violations, and fostering a culture of accountability and integrity.

PRACTICAL TIPS FOR NAVIGATING LEGAL STRUCTURES

Navigating legal structures can feel overwhelming, especially when you are starting a business or transitioning to a new structure. To simplify the process, it's essential to break it down into manageable steps and prioritize tasks that will safeguard your business. Here are some practical tips to help you navigate the complexities of legal structures effectively:

1. **Research Industry-Specific Requirements:** One of the most critical steps in choosing a legal structure is understanding the specific legal requirements of your industry. Different sectors have distinct regulations that dictate how businesses should operate, report, and maintain records. For example, healthcare businesses, such as Allstar Community Care, must comply with HIPAA regulations, while a party planning business, like Pinkolicious, might focus more on liability waivers and safety compliance. Conduct thorough research to know what applies to your field. This might involve consulting government websites, industry associations, or legal experts specializing in your niche. Keeping this knowledge updated is crucial, as regulations may change over time.

2. **Invest in Legal Advice:** While it might seem tempting to handle legal setup on your own to save costs, investing in professional legal advice is invaluable. Legal experts can guide you through selecting the right structure, whether it's a sole proprietorship,

LLC, corporation, or partnership. They help you understand the implications of each choice and ensure you meet state and federal requirements. A lawyer can also assist in drafting necessary documents, such as operating agreements and partnership contracts, which protect your interests. Spending a bit more initially can save you from costly mistakes and potential legal challenges down the line.

3. **Prioritize Liability Protection:** Understanding how different legal structures protect your personal assets is fundamental. For example, operating as a sole proprietor means you are personally liable for business debts and legal actions, while forming an LLC or corporation can separate your personal and business liabilities. Assess the risks associated with your industry. For instance, in healthcare, the potential for malpractice claims makes liability protection essential. Ensure that your chosen structure adequately shields your assets, and consider supplemental insurance if necessary.

4. **Document Everything:** Proper documentation is your best defense against legal issues. This means not only maintaining financial records and contracts but also keeping a log of compliance checks, training sessions, and any legal consultations you have. When I transitioned from Pinkolicious to Allstar, I learned the hard way that documenting compliance measures is not just a formality but a necessity. Keep records of licenses, employee certifications, business permits, client agreements, and any updates to company policies. In the event of an audit or dispute, well-organized documents can demonstrate your commitment to compliance and protect you legally.

5. **Build a Compliance Checklist:** Legal requirements are not static; they evolve over time. Therefore, it's important to create a compliance checklist and update it regularly. Start by listing essential tasks, such as renewing licenses, updating liability insurance, conducting staff training, and revising policies in accordance with new regulations. Include specific deadlines and responsible team members to ensure accountability. A well-maintained checklist helps you stay organized and reduces the risk of overlooking critical compliance tasks. To make it even more effective, incorporate it into your project management system or regular staff meetings.

By following these practical tips, you can make informed decisions about your legal structure and maintain compliance with less stress. Establishing a solid legal foundation from the beginning protects your business, minimizes risks, and allows you to focus on growth without constantly worrying about legal setbacks. Taking these steps proactively secures your business and fosters a culture of responsibility and accountability within your organization.

REFLECTION PROMPTS

Reflecting on your approach to compliance is crucial for maintaining a responsible and legally sound business. Taking the time to think critically about your practices not only helps you identify areas for improvement but also strengthens your leadership in fostering a culture of accountability. Consider the following reflection prompts to gain deeper insights into how you manage compliance within your business:

1. **How do you ensure that your team understands the importance of compliance?** Think about the methods you use to communicate compliance expectations to your team. Do you rely solely on formal training sessions, or do you integrate compliance reminders into daily routines and meetings? Consider whether your team truly grasps why compliance is essential beyond just following rules. It may be helpful to evaluate how you present compliance topics—are they viewed as mandatory checkboxes or as critical practices that protect the business and its clients? Reflecting on this prompt can guide you to develop more engaging and informative ways to instill a compliance-first mindset.

2. **Have you ever overlooked a legal requirement that later became an issue?** Honesty is key when reflecting on past mistakes. Perhaps there was a time when you unintentionally skipped a step or overlooked a detail, thinking it wouldn't be significant. Maybe it was something as simple as not renewing a license on time or not updating client consent forms. Acknowledging these instances helps you learn from them. Consider what led to the oversight—was it a lack of awareness, insufficient training, or simply a busy

schedule? Reflecting on the causes will enable you to put preventive measures in place to avoid similar issues in the future.

3. **What steps can you take today to safeguard your business legally?** Taking proactive measures today can prevent future compliance headaches. Start by identifying any areas where your current practices may be lacking or outdated. This could involve reviewing staff training methods, updating internal policies, or consulting with a legal advisor to ensure all your bases are covered. Think about practical steps that you can implement immediately, such as scheduling compliance reviews, conducting a risk assessment, or creating a more structured checklist for routine legal obligations. By taking small but consistent actions now, you build a more secure and resilient foundation for your business.

Taking the time to reflect on these prompts regularly will not only strengthen your business practices but also enhance your leadership skills. Building a culture of compliance requires self-awareness, continuous learning, and a commitment to proactive management. Use these reflections as a tool to align your team and your operations with legal standards, making compliance an integral part of your business identity.

Mindset Check-In

"How committed am I to building a legally sound business? What steps can I take today to strengthen my legal foundation?"

Prayer

Dear God, grant me the wisdom to choose wisely when making legal decisions for my business. Help me remain diligent and proactive in safeguarding my work, ensuring that my efforts reflect both my commitment and integrity. Amen.

FINANCING YOUR STARTUP

"For which of you, desiring to build a tower,
does not first sit down and count the cost?"
- LUKE 14:28

FUNDING YOUR BUSINESS: NAVIGATING STARTUP COSTS AND FINANCING OPTIONS

One of the most daunting parts of starting a business is figuring out how to fund it. Whether you're using your savings, taking out a loan, or seeking investors, understanding your startup costs and funding options is essential. The financial foundation you set at the beginning can significantly impact your business's long-term sustainability and growth. I learned this firsthand when I transitioned from running Pinkolicious Birthday Party Spa for Girls to opening Allstar Community Care.

Understanding Startup Costs

Before launching your startup, it's crucial to have a clear understanding of the costs involved. Estimating your startup costs accurately helps you determine how much funding you'll need and ensures that you're financially prepared. Without this insight, you risk running out of money before your business has a chance to gain traction.

When I decided to move Pinkolicious to a more upscale location, I knew that the rent would triple. My husband was nervous about the financial risk, and we had to drain our savings to renovate the new space. At that moment, I realized how critical it was to assess costs accurately. Despite the risk, I took a leap of faith, and the move paid off. Pinkolicious grew, and the increased revenue allowed me to open Allstar without additional financial stress.

This experience taught me the importance of planning and calculating expenses thoroughly before making big decisions. If I hadn't taken the time to project the costs and weigh the potential benefits, I might have been overwhelmed by the financial burden. It's essential to not only consider the immediate expenses but also anticipate ongoing costs that could arise after the move or expansion.

Steps to Calculate Startup Costs

1. **Make a List of Necessary Expenses:** Start by listing everything you'll need, from legal fees and licenses to office space, equipment, and marketing. Think beyond the obvious. For instance, if your business involves hosting events, factor in insurance, decorations, and staffing.

2. **Separate One-Time Costs from Ongoing Costs:** One-time costs include expenses like furniture, renovations, and equipment purchases. Ongoing costs include rent, utilities, salaries, and maintenance. Having a clear distinction between these two helps you budget more effectively and manage cash flow.

3. **Research Costs:** Don't just guess—get accurate figures. Contact vendors for quotes, look up lease prices, and estimate wages based on local rates. For example, when I moved Pinkolicious, I researched nearby rental costs and calculated the potential revenue increase before committing to the new space.

4. **Factor in a Cushion:** Unexpected expenses are common in business, especially during the startup phase. Add a financial cushion of 10-20% above your estimated costs to cover unanticipated challenges. Whether it's a sudden need for additional staff or unexpected repairs, this buffer can prevent a financial crisis.

5. **Create a Budget:** Once you have your figures, create your budget. Use this budget as a roadmap to stay on track. Regularly compare your actual spending to your budget to identify areas where adjustments are needed.

FUNDING OPTIONS FOR STARTUPS

After calculating your startup costs, the next step is to figure out how to finance them. Your approach may vary depending on your business model, personal financial situation, and risk tolerance.

Bootstrapping vs. External Funding

When I started my first businesses, I relied heavily on bootstrapping—using personal savings and revenue generated from Pinkolicious. At that time, I didn't have access to loans or investors, so I made do with what I had. Bootstrapping taught me financial discipline and resourcefulness, but it also limited my ability to scale quickly.

- **Bootstrapping:** This approach means funding your business with personal savings or revenue. It gives you full control over your business without the pressure of repaying loans or meeting investor expectations. However, it can slow growth since resources are limited.

- **External Funding:** This option involves obtaining capital from outside sources, such as loans, investors, or crowdfunding. It provides more financial flexibility and faster growth potential, but may come with strings attached, like debt repayment or giving up a stake in your business.

Funding Methods I Considered

1. **Bank Loans:** Initially, I considered applying for traditional bank loans. The benefit is that you maintain ownership of your business, but the downside is the risk involved if you can't meet the repayment terms. Loans also typically require collateral and a strong credit history, which might not be feasible for every entrepreneur.

2. **Angel Investors:** Although I didn't personally pursue this option, angel investors can be beneficial because they not only provide funding but also mentorship and guidance. In exchange for equity, you gain access to their business experience and networks. This can be particularly valuable for startups needing more than just capital.

3. **Crowdfunding:** I was inspired by how some businesses used crowdfunding platforms like Kickstarter to validate their product ideas before launching. Crowdfunding is a way to raise small amounts of money from a large number of people, often in exchange for early access to the product or other rewards. It's a great way to gauge interest and build a community around your brand.

4. **Grants and Competitions:** Some businesses, particularly those with a social impact component, may qualify for grants or pitch competitions. Winning a grant or competition not only provides funding without the need for repayment but also boosts your credibility and visibility.

5. **Friends and Family:** While borrowing from friends and family can be a quick way to secure funds, it's important to formalize the arrangement to avoid potential conflicts. Clearly outline repayment terms or equity stakes to maintain transparency and preserve relationships.

Making the Right Choice

Choosing the right funding option depends on your business goals, risk tolerance, and willingness to share control. For some entrepreneurs, maintaining complete ownership is a priority, making bootstrapping the best option. Others may prefer the rapid growth potential that comes with external funding despite the trade-offs.

For me, the decision to bootstrap Pinkolicious came from my desire to maintain full control and operate without the pressure of debt. When it came to Allstar Community Care, I was fortunate to leverage the revenue from Pinkolicious to cover the initial costs, eliminating the need for loans or investors. This experience showed me the importance of building a solid financial foundation early on.

Balancing Risk and Reward

Funding your business is about balancing the risks and rewards of each option. Sometimes, taking a calculated risk, such as relocating Pinkolicious to a more upscale location, can lead to significant growth.

Other times, it might be wiser to maintain a lean approach and focus on organic growth. The key is to carefully assess your financial position, project potential outcomes, and choose the path that aligns with your long-term vision.

By thoughtfully considering your funding options and planning for the financial realities of your startup, you set your business on a path toward stability and success. Whether you choose to bootstrap, seek investors, or apply for a loan, make sure your decision is grounded in a clear understanding of your needs and objectives.

LOCAL NETWORKING AND COMMUNITY RESOURCES FOR FUNDING

One of the most valuable lessons I learned later in my entrepreneurial journey was the importance of leveraging local networking opportunities and community resources to secure funding. For many years, I had focused solely on running my business and hadn't prioritized getting out into the community to network. I was so involved in the day-to-day operations that I didn't realize how many funding opportunities I was missing simply because I wasn't connected.

It wasn't until I started attending local events and participating in community programs that I discovered a wealth of resources. These opportunities were right there in my city, but I had overlooked them because I wasn't actively seeking them out. I found that networking through local government-sponsored economic development programs and small business initiatives opened doors to funding options I hadn't considered before.

Valuable Networking Events and Programs

I recommend looking into your local economic development programs, as they often provide essential resources for entrepreneurs. Organizations such as the Small Business Administration (SBA) and the Small Business Development Center (SBDC) are excellent starting points. These programs often offer workshops on business planning, financial literacy, and how to make your business bankable. They also introduce you to Community Development Financial Institutions (CDFIs), which provide funding based on your business's merit and community impact rather than just your personal credit score.

Programs like **Goldman Sachs 10,000 Small Businesses** and local urban leagues also offer training and networking opportunities that connect you with business mentors, investors, and other entrepreneurs. Through these programs, I learned about alternative funding sources that were not dependent solely on my credit but also considered my business's community involvement and growth potential.

Becoming Bankable

One critical aspect of funding your business is becoming "bankable." This means making your business attractive to lenders and investors by demonstrating financial stability and community involvement. Participating in programs like those offered by the SBA and local economic development organizations helps you learn what it takes to become bankable. They teach you how to present your business in a way that builds confidence among financial institutions.

Networking with professionals who have experience securing business funding can provide valuable insights into how to strengthen your financial profile. I found that attending these events not only improved my understanding of financing options but also connected me with people who could vouch for the credibility of my business. Building these relationships can make a significant difference when you're seeking loans or investments.

Key Takeaways

While not every networking event will be relevant, focusing on those specifically aimed at economic development and small business growth can make a substantial impact. I'm not suggesting attending every meet-and-greet or social mixer; instead, prioritize events that are designed to help business owners learn about financial resources and community support.

If I had taken advantage of these opportunities earlier, I could have accessed more financial support when scaling Pinkolicious and opening Allstar Community Care. Now, I actively seek out these programs because they not only provide knowledge but also build relationships that are vital for long-term success.

By integrating local networking and community resources into your strategy, you gain access to funding opportunities that might not be available through traditional banking channels. Making an effort to connect with economic development organizations and participating in targeted networking events can significantly expand your financial options and enhance your business's sustainability.

PITCHING TO INVESTORS

If you decide to seek external funding, crafting a compelling pitch is crucial. Whether you're presenting to venture capitalists, angel investors, or even a potential business partner, your pitch needs to clearly convey your vision and demonstrate your business's financial viability. I didn't pitch to investors when opening Pinkolicious, but I did have to pitch my vision to my husband and convince him that the investment was worth it. Building trust and confidence in your vision is key, whether you're talking to family, friends, or professional investors.

The goal of a pitch is not just to present an idea but to instill confidence that your business will succeed. You need to demonstrate a thorough understanding of your market, articulate how your business will generate revenue, and outline the steps you'll take to achieve profitability. This is where financial metrics become invaluable. They give potential investors a snapshot of your business's potential for growth and sustainability.

Preparing Your Pitch

Start by clearly articulating your business idea and its value proposition. Investors need to understand why your product or service is unique and how it solves a specific problem. Back up your claims with data gathered from market research, showing that there is a demand for your offering. Use visuals, such as graphs or charts, to make your data more digestible.

Explain your business model in simple terms. How will your company make money? Outline your primary revenue streams, whether it's product sales, subscriptions, or service fees. Be transparent about your costs and demonstrate that you have a plan to manage expenses efficiently. Investors appreciate honesty about challenges as long as you also present well-thought-out solutions.

Key Financial Metrics to Include in Your Pitch

Investors want to see that you have a clear financial plan. Here are the key financial metrics that can make your pitch more convincing:

1. **Revenue Projections:** Show how your business will grow over time. Create realistic projections that take into account industry trends, market conditions, and your expected growth rate. Break down your revenue streams and demonstrate how they will evolve as your customer base expands.

2. **Customer Acquisition Cost (CAC):** Calculate how much it costs to gain a customer. This includes marketing expenses, sales team salaries, and any other costs directly related to customer acquisition. Lowering CAC over time shows that your business is becoming more efficient in attracting new clients.

3. **Lifetime Value (LTV):** Estimate the total revenue from a customer relationship. LTV helps investors understand the long-term profitability of your business. Comparing LTV to CAC also demonstrates whether your customer acquisition strategy is sustainable. A high LTV compared to CAC indicates a profitable model.

4. **Gross Margin:** Demonstrates profitability potential by showing the difference between revenue and the cost of goods sold (COGS). A healthy gross margin indicates that your business model can generate profit after covering direct costs. Investors often look for businesses with scalable models that maintain or improve gross margins as they grow.

5. **Burn Rate:** Monitor how quickly you're spending funds. The burn rate tells investors how long your current funding will last. A high burn rate without a clear path to increased revenue can be a red flag, so emphasize any cost-cutting measures you're implementing.

6. **Breakeven Point:** Understand when your business will become profitable. Demonstrating your breakeven analysis shows that you've calculated how long it will take to cover initial investments and begin generating profit. Include scenarios with varying levels of revenue and expense changes to show your preparedness for different outcomes.

7. **Runway:** Calculate how long you can operate with existing funds. This metric is particularly important for startups that are not yet profitable, as it reassures investors that you have sufficient financial resources to sustain operations while executing your growth strategy.

Storytelling in Your Pitch

Numbers alone are not enough to win over investors. You need to connect on an emotional level by telling your story. Share the inspiration behind your business and the problem you're passionate about solving. Explain why you are the right person to lead this venture and how your unique experiences have prepared you for this journey.

For example, when I moved Pinkolicious to a more upscale location, I had to convince my husband that the investment was worthwhile. I didn't just present numbers—I shared my vision of creating a premier party spa where every little girl would feel like a princess. I explained how moving to a better location would not only attract more clients but also establish Pinkolicious as the go-to spot for high-quality children's parties. My passion and confidence helped build trust, making the investment seem less risky.

Practice and Prepare for Questions

Be prepared to answer tough questions. Investors might challenge your revenue assumptions, question your market research, or inquire about your contingency plans. Practice your pitch with mentors or fellow entrepreneurs to get feedback and refine your presentation. The more confident and prepared you are, the more likely you are to make a strong impression.

Local Networking to Strengthen Your Pitch

As I mentioned earlier, participating in local economic development programs and networking events can also help you fine-tune your pitch. Engaging with business mentors, attending workshops, and gaining insights from fellow entrepreneurs can strengthen your presentation. Programs like the **Small Business Administration (SBA)**, **SBDC**, and **Goldman Sachs 10,000 Small Businesses** not only teach you how to structure your pitch but also connect you with potential investors or partners.

Networking with seasoned entrepreneurs can also provide valuable feedback on your financial metrics. They may point out areas you hadn't considered or suggest ways to improve your profitability projections. Additionally, some local business incubators offer pitch competitions where you can practice and potentially win funding.

Financing a startup requires planning, faith, and resilience. Whether you choose to bootstrap or seek external funding, the goal is to strike a balance between risk and opportunity. My journey has shown that preparation and faith can turn daunting challenges into opportunities for growth. Be clear about your financial projections, honest about potential risks, and confident in your vision.

Remember that securing funding is not just about the money—it's about demonstrating that you have a viable, sustainable business plan. By clearly presenting your metrics, sharing your story, and showing your commitment to success, you can inspire confidence in potential investors. Stay adaptable, keep learning, and leverage local networking opportunities to build lasting relationships that can support your business's growth.

REFLECTION PROMPTS

1. What are your estimated startup costs, and how can you minimize them?

_____

_____

_____

_____

_____

2. Which funding method aligns best with your vision and goals?

_____

_____

_____

_____

_____

3. How can you build financial resilience if your initial funding plan falls short?

Mindset Check-In

"Am I being realistic about my startup costs and funding needs? How can I be resourceful in seeking financial support?"

Prayer

Lord, thank You for providing the vision and the resources I need to build my business. Help me to be wise in managing finances, and give me the courage to take calculated risks. Grant me discernment in choosing the right funding path and guide me as I take steps toward success. Amen.

CHAPTER

BUILDING YOUR BRAND

"A good name is more desirable than great riches;
to be esteemed is better than silver or gold."
- PROVERBS 22:1

BUILDING A BRAND: CREATING A MEMORABLE AND MEANINGFUL PRESENCE

Building a brand is about more than just having a catchy name or a professional logo. It's about creating a presence that resonates with people and makes them feel something. Your brand tells a story—it's the story of your business, your values, and the experience you create for your customers. It's about crafting an identity that people can connect with and remember long after they've interacted with your product or service.

A brand is not just a visual element or a clever tagline; it's an emotional connection. When customers see your logo or hear your business name, they should immediately recall the feelings and experiences associated with your brand. Whether it's trust, excitement, luxury, or comfort, the essence of your brand should be consistently conveyed across every touchpoint.

A well-thought-out brand establishes a sense of connection, loyalty, and lasting impact.

Think of branding as the DNA of your business. It's the set of characteristics that define who you are, what you stand for, and how you are perceived in the marketplace. Your brand should reflect your values, your mission, and the unique qualities that set you apart from your competitors. Crafting a strong brand identity requires intentionality, creativity, and a deep understanding of your audience.

As I continued to build and refine my brand, I realized that truly understanding branding went beyond aesthetics and catchy slogans. It required a strategic approach that aligned vision with consistent execution. This insight led me to explore the deeper concepts of branding and how to sustain it through changing times.

Why Branding is Critical to Your Startup's Success

Branding plays a vital role in the success of any startup. It's not just a surface-level aspect of business; it's foundational. Here are some key reasons why building a strong brand is crucial:

1. **Builds Customer Trust and Loyalty:** A well-crafted brand fosters trust and loyalty among your customers. When people recognize and resonate with your brand, they are more likely to choose your product over others. Customers tend to stick with brands that consistently deliver on their promises. For instance,

think about why people remain loyal to well-known brands like Apple or Nike—they trust that the quality and experience will meet their expectations every time. Your brand's consistency in quality, messaging, and customer service builds that same level of loyalty.

2. **Establishes Market Differentiation:** Your brand helps distinguish your startup from competitors. In crowded markets, businesses with a strong, unique brand stand out. Without clear branding, you risk blending into a sea of similar businesses. Branding allows you to communicate your unique selling points effectively. Whether it's your values, your story, or your approach to customer care, your brand identity highlights what makes you different. This differentiation becomes even more critical when competitors offer similar products or services.

3. **Attracts Ideal Customers:** Branding allows you to shape how your business is perceived and attract the kind of customers you want to serve. When your brand clearly communicates your mission and values, it naturally draws in those who resonate with your message. For example, if your brand promotes sustainability, you're more likely to attract eco-conscious customers who appreciate your commitment. This targeted approach ensures that you are not just attracting any customers but the right ones who align with your vision.

4. **Enables Higher Pricing:** A strong brand often allows businesses to charge premium prices because customers are willing to pay more for perceived value and trust. Think of luxury brands like Chanel or Mercedes-Benz—they charge more because their brand identity signifies quality, exclusivity, and prestige. Similarly,

when your brand is seen as reliable, reputable, and high-quality, customers perceive the value as worth the cost. This perception allows you to position your offerings at a higher price point without losing customer interest.

ELEMENTS OF A BRAND

Building a strong brand requires careful consideration of several key elements. Each of these elements contributes to how your audience perceives and remembers your brand. A well-crafted brand doesn't just happen—it's intentionally designed to communicate your values, mission, and unique selling points. Here are the fundamental elements to focus on:

1. **Name:** The name of your brand should be memorable and reflective of your mission. It's often the first impression potential customers have, so it needs to be both catchy and meaningful. A strong name hints at what your business does or the experience it offers. For example, **Pinkolicious Birthday Party Spa for Girls** instantly conveys a playful, fun, and girly vibe, perfectly suited for a spa-themed party venue. The name itself sets the tone for the entire customer experience.

2. **Logo:** Your logo serves as a visual representation of your brand. It should be visually appealing, simple, and consistent across all your branding materials. A good logo is versatile enough to look great on everything from business cards to social media posts. It should also be timeless, avoiding trends that might make it look outdated within a few years. For **Allstar Community Care**, I wanted the logo to evoke professionalism, warmth, and safety. We chose calm,

inviting colors and a clean, modern design to communicate our commitment to community support.

3. **Tagline:** A tagline is a brief, catchy phrase that captures your business's essence. It's a powerful way to communicate your brand's core message. A great example is the Pinkolicious tagline: **"Where every little girl is treated like the princess that they are."** This phrase not only captures the spa's mission but also sets expectations for the experience. A strong tagline should be memorable, concise, and emotionally resonant, reinforcing the brand's promise.

4. **Colors:** The color palette you choose should align with the emotions you want your brand to evoke. Colors are powerful psychological triggers. For instance, soft pastels at Pinkolicious convey a playful, dreamy atmosphere, while blues and greens at Allstar signify tranquility and professionalism. Choosing colors that reflect your brand's personality helps create a cohesive visual identity and makes your branding more recognizable.

5. **Voice:** Your brand voice is how you communicate with your audience. It should be consistent and represent your brand's personality. For instance, the voice I use for **The CEOspeaks** is motivational, candid, and empowering. On the other hand, the voice for **Allstar Community Care** is compassionate, reassuring, and supportive. Maintaining a consistent tone across all platforms—whether in social media posts, customer service interactions, or marketing materials—helps build familiarity and trust.

THE VISION BEHIND PINKOLICIOUS

When I started **Pinkolicious Birthday Party Spa for Girls**, I wanted more than just a business where little girls could celebrate their birthdays. I envisioned a place where every little girl felt like a princess. My daughter's upcoming birthday was the initial spark of inspiration, but it was about more than just one special day. I wanted to create an experience that was memorable, exciting, and full of joy. That vision guided every decision I made, from the decor to the way we treated our young guests.

From the moment families walked through the door, I wanted them to feel like they were entering a magical, whimsical space where their daughters would be pampered and celebrated. It wasn't just about offering a party—it was about providing an experience. That mindset influenced the choice of colors, the decor themes, and even the staff training. We wanted every interaction to reflect our commitment to making every little girl feel truly special.

The tagline, **"Where every little girl is treated like the princess that they are,"** wasn't just a catchy phrase—it was our promise. It encapsulated the essence of what Pinkolicious stood for: celebrating young girls in a way that made them feel cherished and royal. The brand was built around creating that magical, feel-good experience that parents wanted for their children.

Crafting the Brand Experience

To build a brand that resonates, I knew I needed to focus on the little details that make a big difference. From the moment guests arrived, they were greeted with a warm, friendly welcome. The decor was intentionally designed to be bright, colorful, and elegant, giving a sense of stepping into a fairy tale. The staff dressed in coordinated outfits that matched the theme of the day, reinforcing the brand's identity through visual consistency.

We also paid attention to sensory elements. Soft, uplifting music played in the background, and the scent of sweet, subtle fragrances filled the air. The party packages were thoughtfully curated to offer a complete experience, from pampering spa treatments to themed crafts. By aligning every element with the brand's promise, we ensured that the entire experience was cohesive and memorable.

I realized that brand consistency was crucial. Whether it was the way we answered the phone, how we presented our social media posts, or how we decorated the party rooms, it all needed to align with the Pinkolicious identity. Customers could sense when something didn't quite fit, so maintaining that consistency became a top priority.

The Emotional Connection

A strong brand doesn't just attract customers; it builds a loyal community. One of the most rewarding moments was when parents told me that their daughters talked about their Pinkolicious party for weeks afterward. They would share photos online, tagging the business and praising the experience. That kind of organic promotion came from building genuine connections.

Parents didn't just see Pinkolicious as a place to host a party—they saw it as part of their child's special memories. That emotional connection made them return year after year and recommend the experience to others. Building a brand that resonates means creating a feeling that lingers, and that's what made Pinkolicious successful.

Staying True to Your Brand

As Pinkolicious grew, I faced the temptation to expand into other services that didn't quite fit the brand's identity. I considered offering events for older children or branching into more general party themes. However, I realized that doing so would dilute what made Pinkolicious unique. Staying true to the brand meant keeping our focus on making little girls feel like princesses.

That clarity helped guide decisions about partnerships and promotions as well. I was approached by vendors who wanted to offer unrelated products at our events, but I knew that would compromise the brand image. Instead, I chose collaborations that complemented our princess theme and enhanced the experience for our guests.

Maintaining brand integrity also meant training my staff to embody the brand's values. We emphasized kindness, attentiveness, and creativity in every interaction. Customers often commented on how warm and welcoming the environment felt, which reinforced the sense of belonging that Pinkolicious aimed to create.

CREATING A BRAND IDENTITY FOR ALLSTAR COMMUNITY CARE

When I was building **Allstar Community Care**, I wanted to make sure that our brand represented safety, healing, and community. The goal was to create an atmosphere where clients felt supported and valued. Every aspect of the branding had to reflect these core principles, from the visual elements to the way we communicated with clients. Consistency was key.

Visual Branding

One of the first steps was designing a logo that conveyed professionalism and warmth. I chose a calm and inviting color palette to signify a safe, therapeutic environment. Blue and green were prominent because they evoke feelings of tranquility and health. The logo itself was kept simple and clean to reflect clarity and trust. In healthcare, where clients might already feel vulnerable, it was crucial that the brand appeared approachable and comforting rather than clinical or intimidating.

The visual branding also extended to the physical environment of our offices. We used soft lighting, comfortable seating, and artwork that aligned with the brand's message of healing and peace. Clients often mentioned that walking into our space felt welcoming and calming— exactly the reaction we aimed for. This alignment between our visual identity and the client experience reinforced the brand's promise.

Brand Voice and Messaging

Beyond visuals, the way we communicated was equally important. I crafted a brand voice that was compassionate, supportive, and understanding. Whether it was through social media posts, client communications, or community outreach, we maintained a tone that made people feel heard and respected. This consistent messaging helped build a reputation of empathy and reliability.

We also focused on storytelling as part of our branding strategy. Sharing stories of resilience and recovery showcased our commitment to helping people navigate difficult times. By highlighting real experiences, we not only humanized the brand but also inspired trust. People knew that we were genuinely invested in their well-being, not just providing a service.

Building Emotional Connections

A crucial part of branding is making emotional connections with your audience. At Allstar, we wanted to be more than just a healthcare provider—we aimed to be a pillar of support in the community. We participated in local events, sponsored wellness workshops, and partnered with other organizations to expand our impact. Clients appreciated seeing us involved and actively contributing to the community, which strengthened their sense of connection to the brand.

Maintaining Brand Consistency

Consistency is essential in branding. We ensured that every piece of content, from brochures to online posts, reflected the same values. Training staff to embody the brand's principles in their interactions with clients was equally important. A single inconsistent experience could undermine the trust we had worked so hard to build.

LESSONS LEARNED

Building a brand is not a one-time effort. It's a continuous process of refining how you present your business and ensuring that your message remains clear and consistent. Building a brand identity takes thoughtful planning and ongoing commitment. It's not just about creating a logo or choosing colors—it's about ensuring that every aspect of your business reflects your core values. Whether it's through visual design, customer interactions, or community involvement, every detail contributes to how people perceive your brand.

One of the key lessons I learned was the importance of listening to customer feedback. Sometimes, small adjustments can make a big difference in how customers perceive the experience. Listening to feedback from clients helped us fine-tune our approach and maintain relevance.

I also learned that brand loyalty is built through authenticity. When customers believe in your brand and see that you genuinely care about delivering on your promises, they become your advocates. Word-of-mouth referrals and repeat customers are some of the most powerful indicators of brand success.

Ultimately, successful branding requires more than just setting initial guidelines. It demands continuous evaluation and adjustment to stay aligned with customer expectations and industry trends.

Key Takeaways

1. **Be Clear About Your Vision:** Know what your brand stands for and ensure that every aspect of your business reflects that vision.
2. **Consistency is Key:** From visual elements to customer interactions, consistency builds recognition and trust.
3. **Create Emotional Connections:** Think beyond the product or service and focus on how you make people feel.
4. **Stay Authentic:** Be true to your brand's core values, even when faced with opportunities that might seem lucrative but don't align with your identity.
5. **Listen and Adapt:** Customer feedback can help you fine-tune your brand strategy and stay relevant.

Building a brand that resonates requires intention, creativity, and a deep understanding of your audience. It's about more than just creating a product or offering a service—it's about building relationships and delivering experiences that people will remember. Pinkolicious became more than just a birthday party venue because we built a brand rooted in making little girls feel special.

Whether you're just starting or looking to refine your existing brand, focus on creating meaningful connections. Be consistent, stay true to your vision, and let your passion shine through every detail. A well-built brand doesn't just attract customers—it inspires loyalty and transforms one-time clients into lifelong advocates.

BUILDING YOUR PERSONAL BRAND AS A FOUNDER

Your personal brand is just as important as your business brand, especially as a founder. Your story, your vision, and your personality all shape how people perceive your leadership and your business. When I started creating content for **The CEOspeaks**, I wanted my message to be empowering and authentic. I knew that sharing my journey—both the wins and the struggles—would make my brand relatable and inspiring to other entrepreneurs.

The goal of building a personal brand is to connect with people on a human level. Your audience wants to know who you are, what you stand for, and what drives you. When I shared my own story of overcoming challenges and building businesses from the ground up, it resonated with those who were navigating similar paths. It's not just about presenting successes—it's about being open about the learning process, too.

Your personal brand should reflect your values and be consistent with your business brand. When people see you embodying the same principles that your business promotes, it builds credibility. For example, **The CEOspeaks** focuses on leadership, entrepreneurship, and personal growth, so I make sure that my own story reflects those themes. Whether I'm speaking at events, creating social media content, or coaching clients, I keep my message consistent and true to my experiences.

Tips for Building Your Personal Brand

1. **Be Authentic:** Share your story and what drives you. Authenticity is powerful because it builds trust and fosters connection. People relate more to real stories than to polished, overly curated content. Share your successes, but also be honest about the hurdles you've faced. For instance, I often talk about the challenges of balancing business growth with family responsibilities. Being real makes your audience feel they're not alone in their struggles.

2. **Engage on Social Media:** Use platforms like Instagram and LinkedIn to share your journey and connect with others. Social media is a powerful tool for showcasing your expertise and engaging directly with your audience. Post content that reflects your personal values and offers insights into your business practices. Regularly interact with comments and messages to build a community around your brand.

3. **Create Thought Leadership Content:** Share valuable insights and advice that position you as an expert in your field. Write blog posts, record videos, or create podcasts that delve into topics you are passionate about. For **The CEOspeaks**, I focus on sharing practical tips for first-time entrepreneurs and those balancing business with personal commitments. Thought leadership content not only attracts followers but also establishes your credibility.

4. **Be Consistent:** Keep your messaging consistent across all platforms. Whether you're on LinkedIn, Instagram, or speaking at an event, your message should align with your brand identity. Inconsistency can confuse your audience and weaken your personal brand. Create a style guide for your content to ensure that your tone, language, and message stay aligned.

5. **Show Vulnerability:** Let your audience see your challenges and how you overcome them. Sharing your struggles humanizes your brand and makes you more approachable. For instance, I've shared about times when I doubted myself or when business decisions didn't go as planned. Instead of weakening my brand, these moments strengthened it by showing resilience and perseverance.

Personal Brand in Action

When I go live on social media or create motivational content for **The CEOspeaks**, I focus on speaking from the heart. I want to encourage other entrepreneurs to take risks, embrace growth, and keep moving forward despite setbacks. By being open and relatable, I build a deeper connection with my audience.

Similarly, when representing **Allstar Community Care**, I focus on conveying empathy and dedication. Whether I'm discussing mental health topics or community support, I make sure that my personal brand aligns with the professional brand of Allstar. This alignment reinforces the authenticity of both my personal and business identities.

FINAL THOUGHTS

Branding is a dynamic process that evolves as your business grows. It requires a clear vision, consistent execution, and an understanding of your audience's needs. By investing in building a strong brand identity, you set the foundation for long-term customer loyalty and business growth.

As your business brand develops, so too should your personal brand as a founder. This is not just about self-promotion—it's about sharing your journey in a way that motivates and inspires others. It's about being genuine, consistent, and thoughtful in how you present yourself. Your personal brand should complement your business brand, reinforcing your mission and vision through your actions and words.

Whether through storytelling, sharing insights, or simply showing up consistently, your personal brand is an extension of who you are and becomes a natural extension of your business. By being intentional and transparent, you not only build your reputation but also establish a loyal following that believes in your vision. Balancing authenticity with professionalism helps create a well-rounded brand presence that resonates with your audience and supports your business's long-term success.

In the next section, we will explore how to sustain your brand through strategic marketing efforts, ensuring that your brand remains strong and relevant even as the market changes.

REFLECTION PROMPTS

1. What message do you want your brand to convey?

_____

_____

_____

_____

_____

2. How can you ensure consistency across your branding elements?

_____

_____

_____

_____

_____

3. What personal stories can you share to strengthen your brand's connection with your audience?

_____

_____

_____

_____

_____

_____

Mindset Check-In

"Am I allowing my brand to genuinely reflect who I am and what my business represents? How can I make my brand more personal and relatable?"

Prayer

Lord, guide me as I build my brand to reflect the mission and purpose You have given me. Help me to be authentic and consistent in representing my business and my values. Grant me the wisdom to create a brand that honors You and serves others well. Amen.

MARKETING AND GROWING YOUR STARTUP

"Commit to the Lord whatever you do,
and he will establish your plans."
- PROVERBS 16:3

THE POWER OF MARKETING AND BRANDING

Marketing your startup is more than just promoting your products or services; it's about building relationships and establishing a brand that resonates with your audience. Successful marketing is rooted in understanding who your customers are, what they value, and how you can meet their needs in a way that stands out. In this chapter, we will explore how to effectively market your startup, build a strong brand presence, and leverage growth strategies to drive long-term success.

Marketing and branding go hand in hand. While marketing is about creating awareness and generating interest, branding is about establishing a unique identity that leaves a lasting impression. Your brand is the story people tell about your business when you're not in the room. It's the feeling they get when they see your logo or hear your name. Effective marketing amplifies that brand story, ensuring it reaches the right audience in a way that feels authentic and engaging.

Why Marketing Matters

For startups, marketing is not just a task to check off the list—it's a vital component of your business strategy. Unlike established companies with vast resources and brand recognition, startups need to be more intentional and strategic in their marketing efforts. The goal is not only to attract customers but also to build relationships that translate into loyalty and advocacy.

One of the biggest challenges I faced when starting my businesses was figuring out how to stand out in a crowded market. Pinkolicious was not the only party venue in town, and Allstar Community Care was not the only mental health provider. What set my businesses apart was the way I marketed them. I didn't just sell services; I sold experiences. I focused on storytelling, community involvement, and consistent branding to create a sense of connection and trust.

Building Your Brand Presence

To effectively market your startup, you must first establish a strong brand presence. This involves defining your brand's core values, mission, and personality. Your brand presence is how people perceive your business based on every interaction they have with it, whether online, in person, or through word-of-mouth.

When I launched **Pinkolicious Birthday Party Spa for Girls**, my goal was to create a space where every little girl felt like a princess. I designed marketing materials that reflected this magical, whimsical theme, from social media posts to party invitations. The branding was consistent and intentional, reinforcing the idea that Pinkolicious was not just a party venue—it was an experience.

With **Allstar Community Care**, the focus was on safety, healing, and community support. Marketing efforts highlighted our commitment to creating a welcoming environment for individuals seeking mental health services. The branding emphasized trust, professionalism, and compassion, which resonated with clients looking for a safe and supportive space.

CRAFTING A MARKETING STRATEGY

Marketing your startup requires a multi-faceted approach. Start by identifying your target audience. Who are they? What problems do they face, and how can your product or service be the solution? Once you have a clear understanding, craft messages that speak directly to their needs and aspirations.

Your marketing strategy should include:

1. **Social Media Presence:** Engage your audience through platforms like Instagram, Facebook, LinkedIn, and TikTok. Share behind-the-scenes content, customer testimonials, and insights related to your industry.

2. **Content Marketing:** Create valuable content that positions you as an expert. This could include blog posts, videos, podcasts, or newsletters.

3. **Community Engagement:** Host events, sponsor local activities, or partner with other businesses to increase visibility.
4. **Email Marketing:** Build a mailing list to keep your audience informed about new offerings, promotions, and company updates.
5. **Paid Advertising:** Utilize targeted ads on social media and search engines to expand your reach to a broader audience.

Leveraging Storytelling in Marketing

One of the most effective ways to connect with your audience is through storytelling. People tend to remember stories more vividly than facts or statistics. Your brand story should be central to your marketing strategy. Share your journey, your mission, and the reasons behind your business decisions.

When I introduced **The CEOspeaks**, I shared my personal story of being a first-generation entrepreneur navigating challenges while building a legacy. This storytelling approach resonated with aspiring business owners who saw themselves reflected in my journey. Instead of just presenting myself as a coach, I positioned myself as someone who had walked the path they were on—a relatable and credible guide.

GROWTH STRATEGIES FOR STARTUPS

Marketing is not just about gaining initial traction; it's about sustaining growth. Implementing scalable strategies ensures that your efforts continue to yield results as your business expands. Some key growth strategies include:

1. **Referral Programs:** Encourage satisfied customers to refer friends and family by offering incentives, such as discounts or freebies.

2. **Collaborations:** Partner with complementary brands to tap into each other's audiences.

3. **User-Generated Content:** Encourage customers to share their experiences on social media. Repost and credit them to build community engagement.

4. **Data-Driven Marketing:** Use analytics to track which strategies are working and optimize your approach based on the results.

5. **Loyalty Programs:** Reward repeat customers with perks, discounts, or exclusive content.

Measuring Marketing Success

To ensure that your marketing efforts are effective, establish key performance indicators (KPIs) that align with your goals. These might include:

1. **Customer Acquisition Cost (CAC):** How much it costs to gain a new customer.

2. **Customer Retention Rate:** How many customers return after their first purchase.

3. **Social Media Engagement:** Likes, comments, shares, and overall reach.

4. **Website Traffic and Conversion Rates:** How many visitors take a desired action, like signing up or making a purchase.

5. **Return on Investment (ROI):** The financial gain from marketing compared to the amount spent.

Regularly reviewing these metrics allows you to adjust your strategies and focus on what is driving results.

UNDERSTANDING YOUR TARGET AUDIENCE

Knowing who your target audience is can make or break your marketing efforts. To effectively reach your audience, you need to understand their needs, preferences, and habits. Marketing without a clear understanding of your audience can result in wasted resources and missed opportunities. On the other hand, targeted marketing allows you to craft messages that resonate, build stronger connections, and increase customer loyalty.

The process of defining your target audience begins with research, which involves gathering data on demographics, psychographics, buying behaviors, and pain points. Once you have a clear picture, you can create buyer personas—semi-fictional representations of your ideal customers. These personas help guide your marketing strategies and ensure that your messages align with the specific needs of those you're trying to reach.

Creating Buyer Personas

Buyer personas are essential tools in marketing strategy. They help you move beyond vague generalizations and focus on real-world characteristics that define your audience. Each persona should include:

1. **Demographic Information:** Age, gender, income level, education, occupation.
2. **Psychographics:** Values, interests, lifestyle choices, personality traits.
3. **Pain Points:** The challenges or problems they face that your product or service can address.
4. **Buying Behaviors:** How they prefer to shop (online vs. in-store), decision-making processes, and influences.

5. **Goals and Motivations:** What drives their purchasing decisions, and how your offering aligns with their aspirations.

For example, if your business is a wellness center, one persona might be a busy professional in their 30s who values self-care but struggles to find time for it. Another could be a retiree looking for ways to stay active and engaged. Each persona would respond to different messaging and marketing approaches.

PERSONAL MARKETING EXPERIENCE: PINKOLICIOUS & ALLSTAR

Building a business from the ground up often requires creativity and resourcefulness, especially when funds are limited. When I launched **Pinkolicious Birthday Party Spa for Girls**, I had to make every dollar count. Marketing on a shoestring budget pushed me to think outside the box and connect with my community in meaningful ways.

The Pinkolicious Approach

At the start, I couldn't afford professional graphic designers or marketing firms, so I took matters into my own hands. I designed my own flyers, created the logo, and built the website from scratch. I didn't have a background in graphic design, but I was determined to make Pinkolicious look professional and appealing. The logo needed to capture the fun, playful spirit of the spa while also being memorable and unique.

One of my most effective marketing strategies was hands-on community engagement. I visited local schools, daycare centers, and community events to hand out brochures and introduce myself. This direct approach helped me build relationships and made Pinkolicious feel personal and approachable. I wanted potential customers to see that the owner was involved and genuinely invested in making their children's birthdays special.

One of my most memorable guerrilla marketing efforts involved putting together gift baskets using items from the Dollar Tree. I carefully selected small, cute items that matched the Pinkolicious theme, added some branded stickers, and delivered the baskets to nearby businesses. Although the baskets were inexpensive to make, they had a significant impact. People appreciated the thoughtful gesture, and it kept the Pinkolicious name fresh in their minds.

Another key strategy was leveraging social media early on. I posted photos from parties, shared behind-the-scenes content, and engaged with followers regularly. This helped build an online community that matched the local connections I was creating in person.

The Allstar Community Care Approach

When starting **Allstar Community Care**, I applied the same level of resourcefulness. Even though the branding was entirely different— more focused on safety, healing, and community support—I still needed to make every marketing effort count. Just like with Pinkolicious, I designed brochures, created the company logo, and built the website myself. Keeping costs low while maintaining a professional appearance was crucial.

To reach potential clients and referral sources, I took a personal approach. I visited doctors' offices, local clinics, and community centers to introduce the business and personally deliver marketing materials. I explained our services, shared the mission of providing compassionate care, and left behind brochures that clearly outlined what we offered. My goal was to make a lasting impression so they would remember Allstar when their patients needed mental health support.

I also leaned into storytelling as a branding tool. Sharing the story of why I started Allstar helped build connections. People responded to the narrative of wanting to create a safe and supportive environment for those in need. Instead of just promoting services, I focused on communicating the heart behind the brand. This approach resonated with both clients and healthcare professionals, fostering trust and loyalty.

Key Takeaways from My Marketing Journey

Both Pinkolicious and Allstar required a creative, hands-on approach to marketing, but the messaging and methods were distinct. With Pinkolicious, the focus was on joy, celebration, and making little girls feel special. The branding was colorful, vibrant, and full of energy. I leveraged community involvement and social media to spread the word, focusing on the excitement of birthday celebrations.

With Allstar Community Care, the message was centered on compassion, support, and creating a safe space. The branding was softer, more professional, and focused on building trust within the community. I prioritized face-to-face interactions and partnerships with healthcare providers to establish credibility.

One critical lesson I learned is that marketing is not a one-size-fits-all process. The strategies that worked for Pinkolicious didn't directly translate to Allstar because the audiences were different.

While Pinkolicious clients were parents looking for unique birthday experiences, Allstar's clients were individuals seeking mental health support or professionals making referrals. Understanding the unique needs of each audience shaped how I crafted my messages and chose my marketing channels.

Moving from Grassroots to Scalable Marketing

As both businesses grew, I had to transition from grassroots marketing to more scalable strategies. For Pinkolicious, that meant investing in targeted social media ads and creating partnerships with local event planners. For Allstar, it involved building referral networks and hosting community wellness events. The transition required maintaining the personal touch while expanding outreach efforts to reach a larger audience.

Understanding your target audience is foundational to successful marketing. Whether your approach is grassroots or more strategic, the key is to create genuine connections through relatable messaging. Start by defining your ideal customer, then craft marketing strategies that resonate with their needs and values.

In the next section, we will explore practical techniques for gathering audience insights and turning that data into actionable marketing strategies.

REFLECTION PROMPT

What low-cost or grassroots marketing strategies could you implement to build community connections and increase your brand's visibility?

_____

_____

_____

_____

_____

_____

_____

_____

_____

_____

_____

_____

Mindset Check-In

Building your brand from the ground up can feel overwhelming. Take a moment to remind yourself that resourcefulness and persistence are your greatest assets. Stay committed to the journey and focus on the impact, not just the effort.

Prayer

Lord, thank you for giving me the creativity and determination to build my business. Help me to continue using my resources wisely and to remain humble and diligent as I grow. Guide me to connect with the right people and make decisions that align with Your plan. Amen.

OPERATIONS AND BUILDING A TEAM

"Commit your work to the Lord,
and your plans will be established."
- PROVERBS 16:3

Starting a business was one thing, but building a team—that was a whole new challenge. When I first opened **Allstar Community Care**, I knew that I couldn't do it all alone. I needed people who were passionate, reliable, and aligned with my vision. Hiring my first employees felt both exciting and daunting. I realized that while my vision was clear, I needed to learn how to share it in a way that would inspire others to come on board and help me build something greater than myself.

The journey of creating a company culture didn't just start with job postings and interviews—it started with understanding the kind of environment I wanted to create. I knew I wanted a space where employees felt valued, encouraged, and invested in the mission. Whether at **Pinkolicious Birthday Party Spa for Girls** or Allstar, I had to build a foundation based on respect, open communication, and a shared sense of purpose.

HIRING YOUR FIRST EMPLOYEES

Hiring the right team members was essential to scaling my businesses. At **Pinkolicious**, I started small, doing most things myself. I created the party packages, handled bookings, and even decorated the space for events. However, when I launched Allstar Community Care, I realized that handling client care, administration, and compliance on my own was impossible. I needed experts—people who could handle billing, client coordination, and therapy sessions.

The first lesson I learned was to be **clear about the role before hiring**. I had to define responsibilities, expectations, and the type of person who would thrive in the role. While technical skills were important, cultural fit mattered even more. I didn't just need competent workers; I needed people who believed in the mission of Allstar and could connect with our clients.

When to Hire:

1. **Workload is Increasing:** If you find yourself or your team stretched too thin, missing deadlines, or unable to focus on critical tasks, it may be time to hire. Delegating tasks to new employees allows you to focus on core areas, such as strategy, business development, and product innovation.

2. **Specialized Skills Needed:** Hiring is essential when specific skills are required that you or your current team lack. For example, you might need a marketing expert, a financial manager, or a software developer with technical expertise.

3. **Opportunities for Growth:** If your business is expanding—whether it's reaching new markets, meeting growing customer demand, or developing new products—hiring more talent can help you seize these opportunities faster.

4. **Financial Stability:** Make sure your business can support the costs associated with hiring. This includes not just salaries but also onboarding, benefits, and equipment. Start by hiring for roles that directly contribute to generating revenue or improving operations.

How to Hire the Right Talent:

1. **Define the Role Clearly:** Before initiating the hiring process, create a clear job description that outlines the skills, qualifications, and responsibilities required for the role. Be specific about what you expect from candidates and how they will contribute to your business.

2. **Use Multiple Recruiting Channels:** Post job listings on job boards, LinkedIn, and industry-specific websites. Network within your industry and reach out to recruitment agencies when necessary.

3. **Focus on Cultural Fit:** Skills and experience are important, but a new hire must also fit in with your company's culture and values. Look for candidates who share your vision, work ethic, and long-term goals. Cultural alignment helps ensure a collaborative and motivated work environment.

4. **Consider Remote Work:** If your business model allows for remote work, you'll have a larger talent pool to choose from. This can reduce overhead costs and attract top talent from different regions.

Navigating Hiring Challenges

Hiring staff comes with challenges, especially when you don't have any managerial experience. Building a team is not just about finding the right skills—it's about understanding personalities and recognizing your own strengths and weaknesses as a leader. One of the biggest lessons I learned was that how you hire and how you fire both play significant roles in shaping your company culture.

When I first started hiring for **Allstar Community Care**, I didn't fully grasp how much personality dynamics could impact the workplace. It wasn't just about qualifications; it was about finding people who aligned with the vision and could work harmoniously with others. I quickly learned that my own leadership style directly influenced how well my team functioned. Initially, I thought that simply hiring skilled professionals would ensure success. However, it became evident that without the right cultural fit, even the most qualified candidates could cause discord within the team.

One of the most common mistakes entrepreneurs make, especially in the early stages, is hiring friends, family members, or people they feel comfortable with. While it seems like an easy solution—bringing in someone you trust—these relationships often turn out to be bad business decisions. I learned this firsthand when I hired a close friend who didn't quite grasp the professional boundaries required. At first, it seemed like a perfect fit since we already had a good personal rapport. However, that comfort level made it difficult to enforce accountability.

When it was time to address performance issues, the personal connection made it uncomfortable and complicated. My friend didn't take feedback seriously, assuming that our friendship would shield them from the consequences. Eventually, it became clear that keeping a friend as an employee was compromising the business's integrity and my leadership credibility. Letting them go was one of the hardest decisions I had to make, but it was necessary for the company's well-being. That experience taught me the importance of separating personal relationships from professional responsibilities.

Another challenge in hiring is finding the balance between being an empathetic leader and maintaining professional standards. Early on, I found myself struggling to be firm because I didn't want to come across as harsh or unapproachable. However, I realized that being clear about expectations and holding people accountable is a form of respect—not only to the employee but to the entire team. Allowing poor performance to go unaddressed sends a message that mediocrity is acceptable, which can demotivate others who are putting in consistent effort.

Hiring without the support of a human resources company or professional guidance can feel overwhelming. As a small business owner, you might be handling recruitment, onboarding, and managing employee performance on your own. You have to be ready for the challenges that come with being both the employer and the business owner. It requires learning about employment laws, understanding how to conduct interviews effectively, and being prepared to navigate conflicts.

One practical strategy I adopted was creating a standardized hiring process. I developed a set of interview questions that not only assessed technical skills but also explored the candidate's values, communication style, and ability to work in a team. I also introduced trial periods for new hires, which gave both the employee and the company a chance to evaluate fit before making a long-term commitment. This approach minimized the risk of committing to someone who didn't align with the company culture.

I also learned the importance of maintaining professionalism even when hiring people I knew personally. Establishing boundaries from the start was crucial. I made it clear that while I valued our personal connection, the expectations at work would be no different from those set for any other employee. Setting these boundaries upfront helped avoid potential misunderstandings and kept the work environment professional.

One key takeaway from navigating hiring challenges is that mistakes will inevitably occur, but it's essential to turn these losses into valuable lessons. I had to accept that not every hire would be perfect and that some decisions would need to be corrected along the way. I learned to be transparent with my team when changes needed to be made, emphasizing that each decision was aimed at strengthening the business and supporting its long-term goals.

Understanding that seasons come and go helped me move forward without dwelling on setbacks. Each hiring mistake became an opportunity to refine my process, whether it was improving how I screened candidates or being more upfront about the realities of the job. I also became more diligent about conducting exit interviews when someone left the team, using their feedback to better understand what went wrong and how to improve moving forward.

Building a resilient team is an ongoing process. As I continued to grow Allstar Community Care, I made a conscious effort to surround myself with people who not only had the necessary skills but also believed in the mission. While there were still challenges along the way, being proactive about addressing issues and learning from past experiences helped me create a more positive and productive work environment.

Navigating hiring challenges is an inevitable part of growing a business. Whether you're bringing on your first employee or expanding your team, being intentional about your hiring practices and learning from setbacks will make you a stronger leader. Embrace the lessons, build on your successes, and continue to refine your approach as your business evolves.

THE IMPORTANCE OF BUILDING A COMPANY CULTURE FROM THE START

At **Allstar Community Care**, I knew that creating a strong company culture from the very beginning was critical. I wanted to attract people who not only brought skills to the table but also aligned with the mission. It wasn't just about hiring qualified professionals; it was about building a team that shared a commitment to community care, healing, and support. Establishing a positive and cohesive culture meant that employees would feel valued, motivated, and genuinely connected to the organization's purpose.

One key aspect of building this culture was fostering a **sense of community among staff**. I knew that if people felt included and valued, they would be more invested in their work and the overall mission. To achieve this, I focused on promoting open communication, organizing team-building activities, and consistently recognizing achievements. Whether through regular team meetings, informal check-ins, or organized workshops, I made sure that everyone had a platform to share their thoughts and ideas.

Open Communication

One of my primary goals was to build a transparent and communicative environment. I encouraged team members to voice their ideas, concerns, and feedback without fear of judgment. I learned that when employees feel heard, it not only boosts morale but also fosters creativity and innovation. To keep communication channels open, I implemented regular one-on-one meetings where staff could discuss their challenges and accomplishments. These meetings became a space where ideas flowed freely, and it helped me stay connected to the team's day-to-day experiences.

Team-Building Activities

To create a supportive atmosphere, I made it a point to schedule team-building activities that went beyond the typical work routine. These activities could range from a simple group lunch to a more organized team workshop focused on developing new skills. One memorable event was a community service day where the entire team volunteered at a local shelter. It not only strengthened our bond but also reinforced the values that Allstar stands for—community, compassion, and care.

Recognition of Achievements

Another vital element in building a positive culture was recognizing and celebrating success. Whether it was a staff member completing a professional certification or successfully managing a challenging client case, I made sure to acknowledge those efforts publicly. I found that celebrating small wins kept the team motivated and fostered a sense of pride in their work. It also encouraged others to strive for excellence, knowing that their hard work would be valued and appreciated.

Learning from Early Mistakes

One mistake I made early on was not being clear enough about **performance expectations**. I assumed that because I was passionate, my enthusiasm would naturally inspire the team. I thought that everyone would automatically understand what was needed simply by observing my dedication. However, I quickly learned that passion alone wasn't enough to convey expectations.

In the beginning, I focused more on motivating the team rather than setting concrete, measurable goals. I realized that while inspiration is essential, employees also need structure and clarity to thrive. When roles and expectations are not clearly defined, it can lead to confusion, inconsistent performance, and even frustration among staff members.

Clarity and Accountability

After noticing some inconsistencies in how tasks were handled, I took a step back to evaluate the root cause. I realized that I needed to provide **clear job descriptions**, outline responsibilities, and set performance metrics. Instead of assuming that passion would translate into understanding, I began documenting expectations and discussing them openly during onboarding and team meetings.

For example, when hiring client care coordinators, I made it a priority to detail their daily tasks, performance goals, and how their role fit into the larger mission of Allstar. I communicated what success looked like in their position, from accurately documenting client interactions to meeting follow-up deadlines. This level of detail helped new hires understand their responsibilities, and it also made performance evaluations more objective and straightforward.

Consistency Matters

I also learned that consistency in leadership is vital. Initially, I would sometimes address performance issues with some staff members while letting similar issues slide with others. This inconsistency led to confusion and even resentment. To correct this, I developed a **standardized performance review process**, where feedback was given constructively and fairly across the board. By applying the same criteria to everyone, I demonstrated that the company values were not just words on paper but actual guiding principles.

Shaping the Culture Moving Forward

Over time, I learned that building a strong company culture is an ongoing process, not a one-time effort. Culture is dynamic—it evolves as the team grows, new challenges arise, and the business landscape changes. I made it a point to regularly revisit our core values and ensure that they were not only stated but actively practiced.

For instance, during our team meetings, I would highlight how specific actions or decisions aligned with our core values. Whether it was a clinician going the extra mile to support a client or an administrative assistant streamlining our scheduling system, I connected these actions back to our culture of **care, efficiency, and community impact**. This practice reinforced the idea that everyone contributes to shaping and maintaining our culture, and it encouraged staff to embody these values daily.

Another key to sustaining a positive culture was involving the team in decision-making processes whenever possible. Whether we were considering new software, revising client intake procedures, or planning a community outreach event, I made sure to gather input from those who would be directly affected. This inclusive approach fostered a sense of ownership and accountability among staff members.

Building a company culture is not just about crafting a vision statement—it's about living that vision every day. It requires being clear about expectations, fostering open communication, and consistently recognizing achievements. By investing in people and prioritizing their well-being and professional growth, I was able to create a team that not only believed in the mission but was also dedicated to fulfilling it.

At Allstar, culture was not an afterthought—it was the foundation. And even when mistakes were made, I saw them as opportunities to strengthen our community and learn together. By being intentional, adaptable, and committed to growth, we built a workplace where employees felt valued and clients felt cared for.

BALANCING LEADERSHIP AND DELEGATION

As my business grew, I learned one of the most valuable lessons of entrepreneurship: the importance of letting go and delegating tasks. Initially, I struggled with trusting others to take over responsibilities. After all, I had built the business from the ground up, and it felt natural to want to oversee every detail. I was used to being hands-on, from planning birthday parties at **Pinkolicious** to managing client care at **Allstar Community Care**.

However, as the workload increased and the team expanded, I realized that trying to do everything myself was not sustainable. Not only did it lead to burnout, but it also stifled the growth of my employees. Building a successful team meant empowering others to lead, not just following my direction.

Learning to Let Go

Letting go was not easy at first. I was accustomed to having full control over tasks, especially those that I felt directly impacted the quality of service we delivered. I feared that if I didn't handle certain tasks personally, they wouldn't be done to my standards. This mindset, however, was holding back both the business and the potential of my team members.

One of the biggest realizations I had was the importance of **understanding my own strengths and weaknesses**. As entrepreneurs, we often feel the need to do it all—wearing every hat, managing every task, and overseeing every detail. However, this mindset can quickly lead to burnout and inefficiency. The reality is that no one is great at everything, and recognizing your own limitations is a sign of growth and maturity as a leader.

For me, one of the areas I've had to be honest about is **customer service**. I know what I want in terms of customer experience, and I have a clear vision of how I want my clients to feel when interacting with my business. I value professionalism, empathy, and timely resolution of issues. However, I also know that my **patience is limited**, and that can make it challenging for me to consistently manage customer interactions, especially when emotions run high or problems arise.

Initially, I tried to handle it all myself—answering phones, addressing complaints, and resolving customer issues. However, I quickly realized that my **short patience** sometimes made situations more stressful than they needed to be. I wasn't providing the level of service I expected, and it wasn't fair to the clients or me. I had to come to terms with the fact that customer service just isn't my strongest suit, and that's okay.

Accepting this weakness didn't mean lowering my standards; it meant finding a **better way** to achieve them. Instead of forcing myself to constantly manage customer interactions, I chose to **delegate this responsibility** to team members who genuinely enjoy helping others and have a natural ability to remain calm under pressure. By hiring people who excel in customer relations, I was able to ensure that my clients received the care and attention they deserved while allowing me to focus on areas where I could truly make an impact.

It wasn't easy to let go at first. I worried that no one else would handle customer issues the way I would. But I had to remind myself that just because someone does something differently doesn't mean they're doing it wrong. In fact, the team members I hired were often more patient, compassionate, and solution-focused than I could be in those moments. Seeing them thrive in these roles was a relief and a revelation.

Training and Mentoring for Success

To effectively delegate, I knew I had to invest time in training and mentoring my team. It wasn't enough to simply assign tasks—I needed to ensure that my staff felt confident and equipped to handle their responsibilities. I developed training modules that outlined standard procedures and best practices for each role. This gave employees a clear framework to follow while also allowing room for personal initiative.

Mentoring became a cornerstone of my leadership style. Instead of micromanaging, I positioned myself as a guide, offering support and advice when needed. I encouraged team members to think critically and devise their own solutions before seeking my input. This not only empowered them but also freed me to focus on strategic planning and business development.

One of the most rewarding aspects of mentoring was seeing my team members grow into their roles. For instance, one of my early hires at Allstar started as a client care coordinator. Through consistent mentorship and training, they eventually took on a supervisory role, helping onboard new staff and managing daily operations. Witnessing this growth reaffirmed my belief that leadership is about building others up, not just overseeing tasks.

Delegating Decision-Making

One of the biggest shifts in my leadership approach was delegating decision-making. Initially, I wanted to be involved in every choice, whether it was selecting new office supplies or deciding on client outreach strategies. However, I soon realized that constantly being the decision-maker was not only exhausting but also discouraged my team from taking initiative.

To address this, I created a decision-making framework. I categorized decisions into three levels:

1. **Low-Stakes Decisions:** Routine choices that could be made independently by team members (e.g., scheduling social media posts or choosing event themes at Pinkolicious).
2. **Moderate-Stakes Decisions:** Decisions that require team collaboration but not necessarily my final approval (e.g., organizing a community outreach event or updating administrative protocols).
3. **High-Stakes Decisions:** Strategic decisions that impact the business's direction or finances, which I would make in consultation with the leadership team.

By clearly defining these categories, I made it easier for employees to know when they could act autonomously and when they needed to consult me. This clarity reduced bottlenecks and fostered a sense of ownership within the team.

The Power of Trust

Ultimately, delegating successfully comes down to building trust. Trusting your team to handle responsibilities doesn't mean abandoning your leadership role; it means equipping others with the skills and confidence to contribute meaningfully. I learned that giving space for creativity and problem-solving not only developed my team's skills but also strengthened their commitment to our mission.

By understanding my strengths and weaknesses, I could make more strategic decisions about which tasks to delegate. For example, letting go of customer service was not a sign of weakness, but rather a recognition that others were better suited for the role. By leveraging their strengths, I could focus on the areas where I could make the most impact.

Through delegation, I was able to focus more on strategic growth rather than being bogged down with daily tasks. I found that as my team grew more competent and confident, I could step back without worrying about every detail. This shift not only benefited me but also empowered my team members to take pride in their work and invest in the company's success.

Learning to let go and delegate was a turning point in my journey as a leader. By trusting my team, investing in their development, and allowing them to take ownership of their roles, I created a more resilient and self-sufficient organization. As the business continued to grow, I realized that empowering others was not just beneficial—it was essential.

BUILDING LEADERSHIP CAPACITY WITHIN YOUR TEAM

As your business grows, it's essential to cultivate leadership skills among your team members. Building leadership capacity is not just about preparing for succession or delegation—it's about creating a resilient organization where responsibility is shared and innovation flourishes. By empowering others to lead, you reduce the risk of burnout for yourself and create a workplace where employees feel valued and invested in the company's success.

Why Building Leadership Capacity Matters

One of the most significant challenges of running a growing business is maintaining consistency and quality as your operations expand. You can't be everywhere at once, and that's why building leadership capacity within your team is essential. Developing leaders from within ensures that your vision and values are upheld, even when you're not directly involved in every decision.

Investing in leadership development also improves employee retention. When people see a clear path for growth within the organization, they are more likely to stay, take ownership of their roles, and contribute to long-term success. Additionally, empowering your team to take initiative fosters a proactive culture where challenges are met with solutions rather than hesitation.

Identifying Potential Leaders

The first step in building leadership capacity is identifying employees who have both the potential and the desire to lead. Not everyone is suited for leadership, and that's okay. Look for individuals who consistently demonstrate the following traits:

1. **Proactive Problem-Solving:** They don't just identify issues— they actively work toward solutions.
2. **Dependability:** They consistently meet deadlines and take accountability for their work.
3. **Positive Influence:** They naturally motivate and encourage others, fostering a collaborative environment.
4. **Willingness to Learn:** They are open to feedback and eager to develop new skills.
5. **Commitment to the Mission:** They align with the company's core values and are passionate about its success.

Once you've identified potential leaders, it's crucial to have a conversation with them about their career aspirations. Some may be eager to take on more responsibility, while others may prefer to focus on their current roles. Understanding their goals will help you tailor your approach to leadership development.

Strategies for Building Leadership Capacity

1. **Mentorship Programs:** Pair emerging leaders with experienced mentors within the organization. This relationship provides guidance, support, and real-world insights into leadership challenges. I've found that mentorship fosters personal and professional growth, creating a strong foundation for leadership development.

2. **Leadership Training Workshops:** Offer training that focuses on key leadership skills such as conflict resolution, team motivation, and strategic thinking. At **Allstar Community Care**, we hosted workshops on effective communication and managing team dynamics, which gave emerging leaders practical tools to succeed.

3. **Delegating Decision-Making:** Start by delegating small but meaningful decisions to build confidence. For instance, allowing team leads to plan staff meetings or handle client feedback independently helps them practice leadership in a controlled environment.

4. **Providing Growth Opportunities:** Encourage employees to take on new projects or lead initiatives. At **Pinkolicious**, I allowed team members to take charge of planning special events, which not only developed their organizational skills but also boosted their confidence.

5. **Encouraging Ownership:** Shift from giving directions to setting goals. Instead of micromanaging, present challenges and ask team members how they would approach the problem. This approach encourages critical thinking and ownership.

6. **Creating a Leadership Pipeline:** Establish clear pathways for promotion and leadership roles. Make it known that growth is not only possible but also expected for those who demonstrate commitment and capability.

Cultivating a Leadership Mindset

Leadership is not just a position; it's a mindset. Encourage your emerging leaders to think strategically rather than focusing solely on day-to-day tasks. Discuss the **bigger picture** during team meetings and ask for their input on long-term strategies. This inclusion makes them feel valued and helps them see how their efforts impact the organization as a whole.

Encourage leaders to practice **emotional intelligence**—the ability to manage their own emotions and understand the emotions of others. This skill is crucial when navigating conflicts, providing feedback, and motivating their peers. Offer resources like books, podcasts, or training sessions on emotional intelligence to build this essential leadership quality.

Coaching and Providing Feedback

Developing leaders requires consistent feedback and coaching. I learned that simply promoting someone to a leadership position doesn't automatically prepare them for the challenges they will face. It's important to provide ongoing support, helping them navigate their new responsibilities while learning from their mistakes.

When offering feedback, focus on growth rather than criticism. Frame your guidance around how they can improve and what they did well.

For example, instead of saying, "You handled that client complaint poorly," try, "Let's discuss some strategies for managing challenging client interactions more effectively next time." This approach keeps morale high while still addressing areas for improvement.

Leading by Example

To build leadership capacity within your team, you must first model the behaviors you want to see. Be consistent, communicative, and willing to admit when you don't have all the answers. Demonstrating vulnerability and a willingness to learn shows your team that leadership is an ongoing journey.

One of the most impactful lessons I learned was that people are more likely to step into leadership roles when they see their leader actively practicing what they preach. Whether it's staying calm under pressure, taking accountability for mistakes, or showing appreciation for hard work, your actions set the standard for how leadership looks within your organization.

Measuring Leadership Success

To ensure your leadership development efforts are working, establish metrics to evaluate progress. These can include:

1. **Team Productivity:** Are leaders effectively motivating their teams to meet goals?
2. **Employee Retention:** Are employees staying longer under supportive leadership?
3. **Problem-Solving Efficiency:** Are leaders independently resolving issues?

4. **Employee Engagement:** Are team members motivated and involved in decision-making?

Regularly assess these metrics and adjust your leadership development strategies as needed. Recognize that not every initiative will be successful on the first try, but by being adaptable, you can continuously improve the process.

Moving Forward

Building leadership capacity within your team is an investment that pays dividends in stability, morale, and sustainable growth. As your organization evolves, having capable leaders in place ensures that your vision continues to thrive, even when you're not directly involved.

Empowering others to lead not only lightens your own load but also builds a more resilient and adaptive organization. Remember, leadership is not about control—it's about enabling others to take ownership and excel in their roles. As your team develops leadership skills, your business will be better equipped to handle challenges, innovate, and expand.

Building and leading a team is one of the most challenging yet rewarding aspects of entrepreneurship. As your business grows, so does the complexity of managing people, delegating tasks, and nurturing leadership within your organization. From learning to let go and delegate responsibilities to cultivating a strong company culture, building a team requires intention, patience, and continuous growth.

Throughout my journey with **Pinkolicious** and **Allstar Community Care**, I learned that successful leadership is not about controlling every aspect but about empowering others to take ownership. By recognizing my strengths and weaknesses, I was able to make strategic decisions about what to delegate and how to build a team that complements my vision. Understanding that no one excels at everything allowed me to trust my team members to handle tasks that didn't align with my strengths, like customer service, while focusing my energy on areas where I could make the most impact.

Building leadership capacity within your team ensures that your business remains strong and adaptive as it scales. By investing in mentorship, fostering open communication, and creating a culture of growth, you lay the foundation for long-term success. Leadership is not just about guiding others—it's about creating a legacy where your vision can thrive even when you're not directly involved.

As you continue your entrepreneurial journey, remember that leadership is an evolving process. Be open to learning from your mistakes, embrace the strengths of your team, and stay committed to building a positive and supportive work environment. Your ability to inspire, delegate, and develop leaders within your organization will ultimately determine your business's resilience and success.

In the next chapter, we will explore the financial aspects of running a business: understanding cash flow, managing expenses, and making strategic financial decisions to ensure your business's sustainability and growth.

REFLECTION PROMPTS

1. Have you considered the values and mission you want your team to embody?

_____

_____

_____

_____

_____

2. How do you ensure that your new hires align with the culture you're building?

_____

_____

_____

_____

_____

3. What lessons have you learned from your first hiring experiences?

_____

_____

_____

_____

_____

_____

Mindset Check-In

"Am I leading by example when it comes to work ethic and commitment? Do my employees see the passion I have for our mission, and am I encouraging them to share that same enthusiasm?"

Prayer

Lord, as I build my team and grow my business, guide me to choose people who align with the vision You've given me. Help me to lead with integrity, patience, and a spirit of collaboration. Bless our efforts, and let our work reflect Your grace and purpose. Amen.

CHAPTER

FINANCIAL MANAGEMENT AND ACCOUNTING

"The plans of the diligent lead to profit
as surely as haste leads to poverty."
- PROVERBS 21:5

SETTING UP A FINANCIAL SYSTEM: A GUIDE FOR NEW ENTREPRENEURS

Starting a business can feel like a whirlwind of excitement, ideas, and a never-ending to-do list. One of the most important yet often overlooked parts of building a successful business is setting up a solid financial system from the very beginning. It might seem daunting, especially if you're not naturally numbers-driven, but establishing a good financial foundation will save you a lot of headaches down the road.

Why a Financial System Matters

Imagine this: You've started your business, clients are coming in, and money is flowing. But suddenly, tax season arrives, and you're scrambling to find receipts, track expenses, and figure out how much you owe. Or worse, you realize your cash flow is tighter than expected because you didn't track your spending accurately.

Having a financial system in place from day one helps you stay organized, compliant, and prepared for growth. It's not just about keeping the IRS happy; it's about ensuring your business is financially healthy and sustainable.

Step 1: Separate Your Personal and Business Finances

One of the biggest mistakes new entrepreneurs make is mixing personal and business finances. You might think, "It's just one account, and I'll sort it out later," but this mindset can lead to confusion and potential legal issues.

Here's What to Do:
- **Open a Dedicated Business Bank Account:** This is non-negotiable. Keep your business income and expenses separate from your personal funds. This not only makes accounting easier but also protects your personal assets in case of legal trouble.
- **Use a Business Credit Card:** Even if you're just starting out, applying for a small business credit card helps build your business credit and allows you to track expenses separately.

What Not to Do:
- Don't swipe your personal debit card for business purchases. It will only make your bookkeeping messy and difficult to track.

- Avoid paying yourself randomly from the business account. Set up a regular payroll or owner's draw to keep things organized.

Step 2: Choose the Right Accounting Method

As a new entrepreneur, you'll need to decide between two accounting methods: **cash accounting** and **accrual accounting**.

Cash Accounting: Records income and expenses when cash actually changes hands. This method is simpler and works well for small businesses with straightforward transactions.

Accrual Accounting: Records income and expenses when they are incurred, even if the cash hasn't been received or paid yet. This gives a more accurate picture of your business's financial health but requires more detailed tracking.

Here's What to Do:
- **Understand Your Needs:** If you're running a small service-based business with few transactions, cash accounting might be sufficient. However, if you're planning to scale or handle inventory, accrual accounting is often better.
- **Get Professional Advice:** An accountant can help you choose the method that best fits your business model.

What Not to Do:
- Don't choose a method without considering how your business might grow. Changing accounting methods later can be complex and time-consuming.
- Don't assume the simpler method is always better—think long-term.

Step 3: Use Accounting Software

Gone are the days of manually recording every transaction. Modern accounting software can save you time, reduce errors, and make financial reporting a breeze.

Here's What to Do:

- **Choose User-Friendly Software:** Start with something simple like QuickBooks, Xero, or FreshBooks. These tools automate tasks like invoicing, payroll, and expense tracking.
- **Automate Where Possible:** Set up recurring invoices and link your bank account for automatic transaction tracking. This will save you hours of manual entry.
- **Track Daily:** Make it a habit to check your financial dashboard regularly. Keeping an eye on your numbers helps you catch issues early.

What Not to Do:

- Don't ignore the software after setting it up. Regular updates are crucial for accuracy.
- Don't skip tutorials or training. Taking the time to learn the software up front will pay off in the long run.

Step 4: Create a Realistic Budget

A budget is your financial roadmap. It guides how you allocate resources, set goals, and prepare for unexpected costs.

Here's What to Do:

- **List Your Fixed and Variable Expenses:** Fixed costs might include rent, salaries, or loan payments. Variable costs, on the other hand, may include expenses such as marketing, materials, or travel.

- **Be Conservative:** It's better to underestimate income and overestimate expenses. That way, you're prepared for the worst-case scenario.
- **Include a Cushion:** Set aside at least 10-20% of your budget for unexpected expenses. It's better to have it and not need it than to need it and not have it.

What Not to Do:

- Don't make your budget too optimistic. Realism is key to staying financially sound.
- Don't set it and forget it. Update your budget regularly to reflect changes in revenue or expenses.

Step 5: Track Your Income and Expenses

When you're just starting, it's easy to think, "I'll remember that expense later," but trust me, you won't. Set up a system from the start.

Here's What to Do:

- **Record Expenses Immediately:** Use your accounting software or a mobile app to log expenses on the go.
- **Categorize Expenses:** Group similar expenses together (e.g., marketing, supplies, travel) for better analysis later.
- **Reconcile Monthly:** Match your recorded transactions with your bank statements. This catches errors and helps maintain accuracy.

What Not to Do:

- Don't wait until tax season to sort through a mountain of receipts. Track as you go.
- Don't assume small expenses don't matter. They add up over time.

Step 6: Hire Help If Needed

If numbers aren't your thing, that's okay. You don't have to do it alone.

Here's What to Do:

- **Hire an Accountant or Bookkeeper:** They can set up your system and manage the ongoing workload.
- **Consult a Financial Advisor:** They can help with long-term planning and tax strategies.
- **Outsource Payroll:** Payroll can be complicated even if you only have a few employees. Let professionals handle it.

What Not to Do:

- Don't try to handle complex accounting yourself if you're not confident. Mistakes can cost more in the long run.
- Don't wait until there's a problem to get help. Proactive management is key.

Your financial system isn't a one-time setup. As your business grows, so will your financial responsibilities. Make it a priority to revisit your system regularly and stay updated on best practices.

Financial management might not feel glamorous, but it's the backbone of a successful business. Getting it right from the start will give you the confidence to focus on what you do best—growing your business. Stay diligent, be proactive, and always keep learning. You've got this!

THE CRITICAL ROLE OF FINANCIAL MANAGEMENT IN YOUR BUSINESS SUCCESS

Proper financial management not only helps in tracking income and expenses but also aids in strategic planning. Having a clear picture of your financial situation allows you to make data-driven decisions that support sustainable growth. Whether you're managing a small business, like Pinkolicious Birthday Party Spa for Girls, or a larger operation, like Allstar Community Care, effective financial oversight can make the difference between thriving and struggling.

Good financial management goes beyond balancing the books; it's about making informed choices that impact every aspect of your business. From budgeting for future projects to ensuring that you can cover daily operational expenses, financial management acts as the backbone of your business strategy. Without it, even the most promising startups can quickly find themselves facing cash flow problems or mounting debt.

As a new entrepreneur, it's crucial to understand that managing finances is not just about keeping records. It's about analyzing those records to gain insights into your business's performance and health. By understanding where your money comes from and where it's going, you gain the ability to predict financial challenges before they arise and make adjustments to your strategy as needed.

Financial management also plays a key role in building credibility. Whether you're applying for a business loan, seeking investment, or simply managing daily operations, having organized and accurate financial data demonstrates professionalism. Investors and stakeholders want to see that you are responsible with your funds and that you have a clear plan for growth.

By prioritizing financial management from the start, you set the foundation for long-term success. It enables you to manage risks effectively, allocate resources wisely, and remain agile in a constantly changing business environment. Ultimately, staying on top of your finances not only supports sustainable growth but also gives you the confidence to make bold, strategic decisions.

ACCOUNTING

Startups typically choose between two accounting methods: accrual and cash, which we have discussed earlier. There is also double-entry accounting. This system is the foundation of modern accounting. In double-entry accounting, every financial transaction affects at least two accounts in your books. For example, when you sell a product, your cash account increases, and your sales revenue account also increases. This method ensures that your accounts always remain balanced and helps prevent errors.

Understanding the Chart of Accounts: The Backbone of Your Financial Management System

A **Chart of Accounts (COA)** is an organized list of every account your business uses to record and track financial transactions. Think of it as the roadmap to your financial data, where each "account" is like a specific category that tells you where money is coming from, where it's going, and how it affects your business's financial health.

Setting up a well-organized Chart of Accounts from the start is crucial because it helps you systematically track your business's financial transactions. Without it, your bookkeeping can become chaotic, leading to errors, confusion, and difficulty in understanding your financial position.

Why You Need a Chart of Accounts:

1. **Organization and Clarity:** A COA provides a clear structure for your financial data, enabling you to categorize transactions in a logical and organized manner.

2. **Accurate Reporting:** By organizing accounts consistently, you can generate accurate financial statements, like Profit and Loss Statements and Balance Sheets.

3. **Tax Compliance:** Having a detailed COA ensures you can accurately track deductible expenses and taxable income, making tax filing smoother and more precise.

4. **Financial Analysis:** With a well-maintained COA, you can easily monitor your financial performance, identify trends, and make data-driven business decisions.

5. **Budgeting and Forecasting:** Categorized accounts help you see where your money is going, making it easier to plan budgets and forecast future expenses.

Breaking Down the Key Components of a Chart of Accounts:

Your Chart of Accounts is typically divided into five main categories: **Assets, Liabilities, Equity, Income, and Expenses.** Each category represents a specific area of your business finances. Let's break down each one:

1. Assets: What You Own:

Assets are resources owned by your business that have economic value and can generate future benefits. They can be both **current assets** (used within a year) and **non-current assets** (long-term use).

Examples of Asset Accounts:

- **Cash:** Money held in your business bank account.
- **Accounts Receivable:** Money owed to you by customers.
- **Inventory:** Products or materials on hand that you plan to sell.
- **Equipment:** Physical items like machinery, computers, or vehicles.
- **Property:** Real estate owned by the business.
- **Investments:** Stocks, bonds, or other financial assets.

Why You Need It:

Tracking assets allows you to know what your business owns, which is crucial for calculating your company's worth. It helps you budget and assess your ability to cover liabilities.

2. Liabilities: What You Owe

Liabilities are debts or obligations that your business needs to pay back. Like assets, liabilities can also be **current** (due within a year) or **long-term** (due after more than a year).

Examples of Liability Accounts:

- **Accounts Payable:** Money you owe suppliers for products or services.
- **Loans Payable:** Outstanding loan amounts.
- **Credit Card Debt:** Balances on business credit cards.
- **Accrued Expenses:** Expenses incurred but not yet paid, like utilities or wages.
- **Taxes Payable:** Money owed to the government for taxes.

Why You Need It:

Liabilities show your business's financial obligations. Monitoring them helps you manage debt responsibly and plan for repayment, which is crucial for maintaining financial stability.

3. Equity: Your Net Worth

Equity represents the owner's interest in the business after all liabilities have been subtracted from assets. Essentially, it's what's left over when you pay off your debts.

Examples of Equity Accounts:

- **Owner's Capital:** Your initial investment in the business.
- **Retained Earnings:** Profits that have been reinvested into the business rather than distributed as dividends.
- **Stock:** If your business is incorporated, this represents ownership shares.
- **Drawings:** The Money the owner takes out of the business for personal use.

Why You Need It:

Equity accounts help track how much of the business you actually own versus what is financed by debt. It's essential for assessing your company's value and understanding how much capital is available for reinvestment.

4. Income: What You Earn

Income accounts track the money your business earns from its operations. This is crucial for understanding profitability and generating accurate revenue reports.

Examples of Income Accounts:

- **Sales Revenue:** Money earned from selling products or services.
- **Service Income:** Fees for professional services rendered.
- **Interest Income:** Earnings from investments.
- **Rental Income:** Money earned from leasing property.

Why You Need It:

Income accounts give you a clear picture of your business's earning power. Tracking income accurately helps you calculate gross profit, monitor performance, and make informed pricing decisions.

5. Expenses: What You Spend

Expenses are the costs your business incurs to generate revenue. Tracking these costs helps you understand profitability and control spending.

Examples of Expense Accounts:

- **Cost of Goods Sold (COGS):** Direct costs associated with producing goods or services.
- **Rent Expense:** Costs of leasing office or retail space.
- **Utilities:** Electricity, water, and other essential services.
- **Wages and Salaries:** Employee compensation.
- **Marketing and Advertising:** Costs associated with promoting your business.
- **Office Supplies:** Everyday items used to run the business.
- **Professional Fees:** Payments to accountants, lawyers, or consultants.

Why You Need It:

Expense accounts help you track spending and identify areas where you can cut costs. Keeping a close eye on expenses ensures that you're not overspending, which directly affects your profit margins.

Tips for Setting Up Your Chart of Accounts:

- **Be Detailed, but Not Overwhelming:** Include enough accounts to cover your needs without creating unnecessary complexity.
- **Group Accounts Logically:** Organize related accounts under parent categories (e.g., group all utility expenses together).
- **Follow a Consistent Numbering System:** Use a numbering scheme (such as 1000s for assets and 2000s for liabilities) to keep accounts organized.
- **Customize for Your Business:** Tailor your COA to reflect your specific operations, whether you're a retail store, service provider, or non-profit.
- **Regularly Review and Update:** As your business grows, adjust your COA to reflect new revenue streams or changes in expenses.

A well-organized Chart of Accounts is the backbone of your financial management system. It helps you categorize transactions systematically, making financial reporting more accurate and insightful. Without a clear COA, your books can become messy and difficult to interpret, leading to poor financial decisions.

Invest time in setting up your Chart of Accounts correctly from the start. As your business grows, maintaining a structured COA will make it easier to analyze financial performance, prepare for tax season, and present your business's financial health to investors or stakeholders.

Properly managing your COA not only supports daily bookkeeping but also sets the foundation for long-term financial success.

Developing a Budget

Creating a budget helps you allocate resources effectively and predict financial outcomes. Start by listing your fixed and variable expenses, projected income, and savings goals. Regularly comparing actual numbers against your budget will help you identify areas where adjustments are necessary.

Managing Cash Flow

Cash flow management is about ensuring that more money comes in than goes out. This requires consistent monitoring and proactive planning. Here are some strategies to maintain healthy cash flow:

1. **Invoice Promptly:** Late invoicing can delay your cash inflow. Set up automated invoicing to streamline the process.
2. **Monitor Accounts Receivable:** Keep track of outstanding payments and follow up promptly.
3. **Negotiate Payment Terms:** Extend payment deadlines with vendors while encouraging early payments from clients.
4. **Maintain a Cash Reserve:** Set aside funds to cover unexpected expenses or downturns.

Financial Reporting and Analysis

Regular financial reporting gives you insight into your business's performance. Key reports include:

1. **Profit and Loss Statement (P&L):** Summarizes revenue, costs, and expenses during a specific period.

2. **Balance Sheet:** Provides a snapshot of your assets, liabilities, and equity.

3. **Cash Flow Statement:** Tracks cash inflows and outflows to ensure liquidity.

4. **Break-Even Analysis:** Determines the point at which revenue covers all costs.

TAX COMPLIANCE AND RECORD KEEPING

Staying compliant with tax regulations is not just about avoiding penalties—it's about building credibility and ensuring the long-term sustainability of your business. When you neglect tax compliance, the consequences can be severe, ranging from fines and interest charges to potential legal trouble. As a new entrepreneur, it's crucial to make tax compliance a top priority from the very beginning.

Why Tax Compliance Matters

Being proactive with tax compliance means keeping accurate records of your business income, expenses, payroll, and tax payments. It also involves filing accurate tax returns on time and adhering to both federal and state regulations. Keeping up with tax obligations demonstrates that you are running a legitimate and responsible business, which is crucial when seeking financing or partnerships.

Here's How to Stay Compliant:

1. **Maintain Detailed Records:** Always keep meticulous records of all financial transactions, including receipts, invoices, and bank statements. Whether you're paying employees, purchasing supplies, or invoicing clients, every financial move should be documented.

2. **Use Accounting Software:** Opt for reliable accounting software, like QuickBooks or Xero, to automatically record transactions and store digital copies of receipts. This makes it easier to track your finances and reduces the risk of data loss.

3. **Understand Your Tax Obligations:** Depending on your business structure (sole proprietorship, LLC, corporation), your tax responsibilities may vary. Consult with a tax professional to understand your filing requirements, including estimated taxes, payroll taxes, and sales tax.

4. **Keep Receipts and Documentation:** In the event of an audit, you'll need to provide proof of income and expenses. Keeping digital copies of receipts and invoices can simplify this process. Use cloud-based storage for easy access and backup.

What Not to Do:

- **Don't Ignore Deadlines:** Missing tax filing dates can lead to hefty fines. Set calendar reminders or use software that automatically calculates and submits tax forms.

- **Don't Discard Old Records:** Keep financial records for at least seven years. This includes tax returns, payroll documents, and receipts, as they may be required during an audit or for tax purposes.

EXPENSE MANAGEMENT STRATEGIES

One of the most common reasons small businesses struggle financially is poor expense management. Controlling your costs not only helps maintain profitability but also keeps your business agile, especially when faced with unexpected challenges.

Why Expense Management Matters:

Managing expenses effectively means understanding where your money goes and finding ways to reduce unnecessary spending. Proper expense tracking also ensures that your profit margins remain healthy, enabling you to reinvest in growth opportunities.

Practical Expense Management Strategies:

1. **Use Expense Tracking Tools:** Apps like **Expensify** or **Zoho Expense** simplify recording and categorizing expenses. These tools can integrate with your accounting software, making it easy to upload receipts and categorize expenses automatically.

2. **Categorize Expenditures:** Group similar expenses under categories like **marketing**, **operational costs**, **payroll**, and **supplies**. This structure makes it easier to analyze where your money is going and identify areas for cost reduction.

3. **Review Monthly Statements:** Set aside time every month to go through your bank and credit card statements. Look for discrepancies, recurring subscriptions you might no longer need, or any unapproved transactions.

4. **Set Spending Limits:** Implement budgets for each category to prevent overspending. For example, allocate a fixed amount for marketing each month and monitor adherence to the limit.

Common Mistakes to Avoid:

- **Overlooking Small Expenses:** Small, frequent purchases can add up quickly. Make sure you account for every dollar spent.
- **Failing to Reassess:** Just because an expense was necessary six months ago doesn't mean it's essential now. Regularly evaluate recurring costs to ensure they still provide value.

Financial Forecasting and Planning

Financial forecasting is a proactive approach to managing your business finances. It involves predicting your future revenue, expenses, and cash flow based on historical data and market trends.

Why Financial Forecasting Matters:

Creating financial projections helps you anticipate challenges, plan for growth, and secure funding. Investors and lenders often require detailed forecasts to evaluate the financial viability of your business. Even if you're not seeking external funding, forecasting gives you a clear direction for decision-making.

Steps to Create Financial Forecasts:

1. **Analyze Past Data:** Look at your previous months' income and expenses to establish a baseline.
2. **Factor in Market Trends:** Consider changes in your industry that may impact your revenue, such as seasonal fluctuations or economic shifts.
3. **Project Revenue:** Estimate how much you expect to earn based on customer trends and planned marketing initiatives.
4. **Predict Expenses:** Account for both fixed and variable costs and include a buffer for unexpected expenses.
5. **Use Scenario Planning:** Create best-case, worst-case, and most likely scenarios to prepare for different financial outcomes.

What Not to Do:

- **Don't Rely on Gut Feeling:** Base your projections on data, not intuition. Overestimating income or underestimating expenses can lead to cash flow problems.

- **Avoid Being Overly Optimistic:** While it's good to plan for success, be realistic about potential setbacks.

BUILDING FINANCIAL DISCIPLINE

Financial discipline means consistently managing your money wisely, regardless of whether your business is booming or facing challenges. It's about making financial management a routine rather than an afterthought.

Why Financial Discipline Matters:

Without discipline, even a profitable business can quickly find itself in financial trouble. Staying on top of your finances helps you avoid debt, maintain good credit, and sustain long-term growth.

Building Disciplined Habits:

1. **Set Financial Goals:** Outline your short-term and long-term financial objectives, such as reducing expenses by 10% or increasing revenue by 20%.
2. **Stick to Your Budget:** Treat your budget as a commitment, not a suggestion.
3. **Regular Financial Reviews:** Monthly check-ins help you stay accountable and allow you to make adjustments as needed.
4. **Track Progress:** Measure your financial performance against your goals and make changes when necessary.

Common Pitfalls:

- **Impulse Spending:** Resist the urge to make unplanned purchases, even when cash flow is strong.

- **Procrastinating Financial Tasks:** Neglecting routine tasks like updating records or paying bills can snowball into bigger problems.

SEEKING PROFESSIONAL GUIDANCE

If managing finances feels overwhelming, don't hesitate to seek professional assistance. Accountants, bookkeepers, and financial consultants can help you establish effective systems, manage taxes efficiently, and provide expert insights into your financial strategies.

Benefits of Professional Help:

- **Accuracy:** Professionals ensure that your records are accurate and compliant.
- **Efficiency:** They save you time by handling complex financial tasks.
- **Strategic Advice:** Financial experts can provide insights that help you optimize cash flow and reduce expenses.

Financial management is not just about crunching numbers; it's about making informed decisions that shape the future of your business. By establishing a solid financial foundation, maintaining diligent practices, and seeking professional guidance when needed, you can ensure your startup's long-term success.

Staying organized, compliant, and proactive with your financial strategies not only safeguards your business but also empowers you to pursue growth opportunities confidently. Remember, building good financial habits today lays the groundwork for a thriving business tomorrow.

REFLECTION PROMPT

Think about a financial decision you made recently.

1. What factors did you take into account?

_____

_____

_____

_____

_____

2. How did you ensure it was the best choice for your business?

_____

_____

_____

_____

_____

_____

3. What would you do differently next time?

_____

_____

_____

_____

_____

_____

Mindset Check-In

As you navigate the world of financial management, take a moment to assess your mindset. Managing money can feel overwhelming, especially when you're juggling multiple responsibilities as a new entrepreneur. It's important to approach financial tasks with a growth mindset, viewing challenges as opportunities to learn rather than obstacles to fear.

Ask Yourself:

1. Am I allowing fear or uncertainty about finances to hold me back from making strategic decisions?
2. How can I shift my mindset from seeing financial management as a burden to viewing it as a tool for building a sustainable business?
3. What small steps can I take today to build confidence in managing my business finances?
4. Am I open to seeking help when financial tasks feel too complex or unfamiliar?

Affirmation:

"I am capable of mastering my business finances. I choose to learn, grow, and build financial discipline to support my vision. Challenges are opportunities to strengthen my skills and secure my future success."

Financial management doesn't have to be intimidating. Take it one step at a time, and remember that building financial literacy is part of your journey as a business owner. You've got this!

Prayer

Heavenly Father, I ask for wisdom and guidance as I manage the financial resources You have entrusted to me. Help me make sound financial decisions that honor You and benefit my business. Grant me discernment to manage my income, expenses, and investments with integrity and foresight. In Jesus' name, Amen.

OVERCOMING CHALLENGES AND AVOIDING PITFALLS

"Consider it pure joy, my brothers and sisters, whenever you face trials of many kinds, because you know that the testing of your faith produces perseverance."
- JAMES 1:2-3

Starting and running a business is no easy feat. The journey is filled with challenges, setbacks, and moments when giving up feels like the easiest option. Whether you're launching your first startup or scaling an existing venture, you will undoubtedly encounter obstacles that test your resilience, problem-solving abilities, and passion for your vision. While the excitement of building something from the ground up fuels your drive, the reality of managing day-to-day challenges can feel overwhelming. However, learning how to navigate these obstacles is crucial for long-term success.

One of the biggest challenges entrepreneurs face is maintaining motivation when progress seems slow or non-existent. It's easy to stay driven when business is booming, but what about when sales are down, customers aren't responding, or your marketing efforts seem to fall flat? In these moments, it's important to revisit your "why." Why did you start this business in the first place? What problem are you solving, and what impact do you want to make? Reconnecting with your purpose can reignite your passion and help you push through tough times.

Another challenge is dealing with financial stress. Many startups struggle with cash flow issues, especially in the early stages. The excitement of launching can quickly give way to the harsh reality of unpaid bills, dwindling reserves, and the fear of running out of money before the business becomes profitable. This financial pressure can make you question whether your dream is worth the risk. To mitigate this stress, it's essential to create a realistic financial plan from the outset. Monitor your expenses, prioritize spending, and seek professional advice when necessary. Remember, financial management is a skill that can be learned and improved over time.

Building a strong support system is another critical element in overcoming challenges. Entrepreneurship can be a lonely journey, especially when you're dealing with setbacks. Surrounding yourself with mentors, fellow entrepreneurs, and supportive friends or family members can make a huge difference. They can offer guidance, share their own stories of overcoming obstacles, and provide emotional support when you feel like quitting. Joining business networks, mastermind groups, or local entrepreneurial communities can also connect you with like-minded individuals who understand your struggles and successes.

One of the most difficult aspects of running a business is knowing when to pivot. Sometimes, despite your best efforts, the original plan just doesn't work. Maybe the product isn't resonating with customers, or the market conditions have changed. Pivoting doesn't mean you've failed; rather, it shows your willingness to adapt and respond to feedback. Successful businesses often undergo significant changes before finding their stride. The key is to remain open to new opportunities and not be afraid to change direction when the data clearly indicates it.

Learning from others' failures can also guide you in your journey. Study businesses that have failed and examine the reasons behind their collapse. Was it due to poor financial planning, a lack of market fit, or internal conflicts? By analyzing these failures, you gain insights into how to avoid similar pitfalls. Additionally, take note of companies that successfully turned their setbacks into comebacks. Whether it's through a strategic pivot or a revamped business model, learning from real-world examples can help you make informed decisions during difficult times.

When challenges arise, it's also vital to practice self-care and maintain a balanced perspective. The stress of running a business can take a toll on your physical and mental well-being. Long hours, financial worries, and the pressure to succeed can lead to burnout. Prioritizing self-care—whether through regular exercise, spending time with loved ones, or simply taking a break—can help you stay mentally strong. Remember that taking care of yourself is not a distraction from your business; it's a necessary component of sustained success.

Resilience is at the heart of entrepreneurial success. You will face rejection, criticism, and unexpected setbacks. Some ideas will fail, and not every venture will be profitable right away. It's essential to develop a mindset that views challenges as opportunities for growth rather than threats to your success. Each problem you overcome builds your confidence and prepares you for future hurdles. Cultivate a positive mindset, stay committed to your goals, and keep moving forward despite the difficulties.

Lastly, never underestimate the power of prayer and faith. For many entrepreneurs, their faith is the foundation that keeps them grounded during turbulent times. Seeking spiritual guidance and placing your trust in a higher purpose can provide the strength to keep pushing forward. Acknowledging that you don't have to carry the burden alone can be a source of comfort and encouragement.

In this chapter, we'll explore common startup mistakes, strategies for overcoming challenges, and how to know when it's time to pivot. You'll learn how to build resilience, stay motivated, and make strategic adjustments when your initial plans don't pan out as expected. Embracing challenges as part of the journey will make you a stronger entrepreneur and lead you to more sustainable success. By learning to navigate the ups and downs with grace and determination, you set the foundation for a business that can withstand the tests of time.

COMMON STARTUP MISTAKES (Lessons from Failed Startups)

Starting a business is inherently risky, and not all startups make it. Learning from the failures of others can provide valuable lessons and help you avoid similar mistakes. Some of the most common reasons for startup failure include poor market fit, financial mismanagement, lack of focus, and premature scaling. By understanding these pitfalls, you can navigate your own challenges more effectively.

1. Lack of Market Need:

One of the most common reasons startups fail is building a product or service that no one needs. Many founders are so passionate about their idea that they overlook market demand. Without a clear understanding of customer needs, even the most innovative products can fall flat.

My Experience:

When I started Pinkolicious, I was so excited to create a unique space for little girls to feel like princesses that I didn't initially consider whether parents would actually pay for the experience. Thankfully, community engagement and testing the concept on a smaller scale helped me realize that the demand was there before I invested too much time and resources.

2. Handling Business Challenges

Every startup faces challenges, and how you respond determines your long-term success. Whether dealing with unexpected setbacks, fierce competition, or periods of slow growth, resilience and problem-solving are key.

3. Staying Motivated:

Running a startup can be overwhelming, especially when things don't go as planned. During challenging times, it's crucial to remind yourself why you started and focus on the bigger picture.

Overcoming challenges and avoiding pitfalls is part of every entrepreneur's journey. By learning from mistakes, staying motivated during tough times, and being open to change, you build resilience and increase your chances of success. Pivoting, when done thoughtfully, can turn a struggling business into a thriving one.

The entrepreneurial path is rarely smooth, but each challenge presents an opportunity to grow. Embrace the lessons, remain adaptable, and keep your purpose at the forefront of your journey. Your commitment to overcoming obstacles will not only build your business but also strengthen your character as a leader.

REFLECTION PROMPTS

1. What setbacks have challenged your motivation, and how did you overcome them?

_____

_____

_____

_____

_____

2. Are there signs that your current business model needs to change?

_____

_____

_____

_____

_____

3. What lessons have you learned from past failures or difficult decisions?

_____

_____

_____

_____

_____

_____

Mindset Check-In:

When facing challenges, do I focus on solutions rather than dwelling on setbacks? Am I willing to pivot when necessary and embrace change as a part of growth?

Affirmation: I am resilient and adaptable. I learn from my challenges and use them as stepping stones toward success.

Prayer:

Lord, I seek Your wisdom as I navigate the challenges of entrepreneurship. Help me to recognize when it's time to pivot and guide my decisions with discernment. Grant me the strength to persevere when obstacles arise and the humility to learn from my mistakes. May my journey reflect Your grace and lead to growth and fulfillment. Amen.

LONG-TERM STRATEGY AND SUSTAINABILITY

"For I know the plans I have for you," declares the Lord,
"plans to prosper you and not to harm you,
plans to give you hope and a future."
- JEREMIAH 29:11

EMBRACING THE JOURNEY AHEAD

As you arrive at the final chapter of this book—and a pivotal milestone in your entrepreneurial journey—it's the perfect moment to pause, reflect, and realign. Starting a business is no small feat. It takes vision, courage, faith, and a deep sense of purpose to step out on your own, especially when the path is uncertain. But sustaining that business, growing it with intention, and building something that lasts? That takes a different kind of strength. It requires strategy, patience, and a commitment to evolve through every season.

In the beginning, your energy is fueled by excitement and possibility. You're building something from the ground up, navigating new experiences, and learning through trial and error. There's a sense of urgency in the early stages—hustling to gain traction, reach your first customers, and figure out what works. That fire is important. But over time, what sustains you isn't just the hustle—it's the discipline. It's the vision that keeps you grounded. It's your ability to shift from reacting to planning, from building to leading, and from surviving to scaling.

This part of the journey is about looking forward with clarity and making decisions that are aligned with your long-term goals. It's about recognizing that every move doesn't have to be fast—but it does need to be intentional. You'll need to prioritize not just profits but purpose. You'll need to create systems that outlive your hustle, delegate to grow, and pour into your team the same way you pour into your business.

And yes, you will be stretched. There will be days you feel unseen, unqualified, and uncertain. But there will also be days when everything clicks—when your ideas turn into income, when your team believes in the mission, and when your business begins to run with rhythm. You'll start to witness the fruit of the seeds you planted during the hard seasons. You'll begin to see the impact you've made in your community, your industry, and your own life.

So, as you step into this next season—one of sustainability, strategy, and scaling—know that your story is still being written. You didn't come this far just to come this far. There is still so much ahead of you. Keep your vision clear, your faith strong, and your pace steady. And most importantly, remember that your business is more than a brand or a building—it's a legacy.

You were called to build. Now, you're being called to lead.

BUILDING A SUSTAINABLE BUSINESS

Sustainability in business means striking a balance between profitability and purpose. In today's socially and environmentally conscious world, aligning your business practices with values that resonate with your customers and community is more important than ever. Building a sustainable business goes beyond financial metrics—it's about creating lasting value, minimizing environmental impact, and fostering positive social outcomes.

At Allstar Community Care, sustainability meant more than just financial stability. It involved building a business model that could withstand changes in the healthcare landscape while staying true to our commitment to community care. One way we ensured sustainability was by investing in staff development. Providing ongoing training and support helped reduce turnover, which not only saved costs but also maintained continuity of care for our clients.

Another important aspect was fostering community partnerships. By collaborating with local organizations and participating in community events, we reinforced our role as a trusted resource. This approach not only strengthened our reputation but also brought in consistent referrals, helping the business grow steadily and sustainably.

To build a sustainable business, start by assessing the impact of your operations, not just financially but also socially and environmentally. Ask yourself: Are we making a positive difference in the lives of our clients? Are we minimizing our environmental footprint? Are we creating an inclusive workplace that values diversity and promotes well-being?

Implement practices that support sustainability, such as reducing waste, using digital systems to minimize paper use, and sourcing supplies from responsible vendors. Additionally, invest in your team's well-being. A motivated and well-supported workforce is crucial for delivering quality services and maintaining a positive work environment.

Financial sustainability also means being prepared for economic shifts. Maintain a financial cushion to weather unexpected downturns, and diversify your revenue streams to reduce dependence on a single income source. At Allstar, we diversified by offering different types of services and partnering with various community programs, which helped stabilize our revenue.

Sustainability is an ongoing commitment, not a one-time initiative. As your business grows, regularly evaluate your practices and remain committed to balancing profit with purpose. By aligning your long-term goals with sustainable practices, you not only ensure your business's longevity but also make a meaningful impact on your community.

FINAL REFLECTION: EMBRACING THE JOURNEY

As you reach the final pages of this book, take a moment to reflect on how far you've come, not just in reading these chapters but in your own entrepreneurial journey. Building a business is no small feat. It requires courage, perseverance, and a firm commitment to your vision.

Whether you're just starting out or have been in the game for years, know that every step you take is a testament to your resilience and passion.

When I look back on my journey, I see a series of highs and lows, victories and setbacks, and countless lessons learned along the way. From starting Pinkolicious Birthday Party Spa for Girls as a creative outlet to founding Allstar Community Care to address a vital community need, every venture came with challenges that tested my resolve. There were moments of doubt, frustration, and even fear. But through it all, I kept moving forward because I knew that giving up was not an option.

One of the most valuable lessons I learned is that resilience is not about never falling—it's about getting back up every time you do. As an entrepreneur, you will face challenges that make you question your path. You may launch a product that doesn't sell, hire someone who isn't the right fit, or invest time and money into a strategy that doesn't work out. These moments can feel defeating, but they are also opportunities for growth and self-discovery.

When I decided to expand Allstar Community Care, I didn't fully understand the magnitude of what I was taking on. It wasn't just about offering more services; it was about building a stronger infrastructure, training staff, and maintaining quality care. In my eagerness to grow, I sometimes overlooked the importance of pacing myself and preparing adequately for expansion. Those early mistakes could have been devastating, but instead, they taught me to plan strategically, communicate effectively, and stay grounded in my mission.

Embracing Imperfection

There's a myth that successful entrepreneurs always know what they're doing. The reality is that many of us are figuring it out as we go. There's no perfect roadmap, no guaranteed formula for success. What sets successful business owners apart is their willingness to keep learning and adapting. I used to worry that not having all the answers made me less capable. However, the truth is that the willingness to learn, grow, and change course when necessary is what builds true leadership.

Don't be afraid to embrace imperfection. Your journey is uniquely yours, shaped by your strengths, weaknesses, and experiences. The beauty of entrepreneurship lies not in achieving perfection but in pushing forward despite the imperfections. Allow yourself the grace to make mistakes, and use those moments as stepping stones to become a stronger, more insightful leader.

Finding Your "Why"

Through all the challenges, what kept me grounded was remembering why I started. For me, it wasn't just about building successful businesses—it was about creating safe spaces, empowering others, and making a positive impact. Your "why" is your anchor. When the days get hard and the road feels endless, return to that purpose. Whether it's providing for your family, serving your community, or pursuing a passion that sets your soul on fire, keep your why at the center of your efforts.

It's easy to get caught up in the hustle and lose sight of your initial motivation. That's why it's essential to pause, reflect, and realign with your mission periodically. Take time to celebrate your achievements, no matter how small. Every milestone is proof of your dedication and hard work.

Leading with Integrity

Success is not just about achieving financial goals—it's about leading with integrity and staying true to your values. People will remember how you made them feel, how you treated your team, and whether your business contributed positively to the community. Never compromise your principles for short-term gains. Building a legacy means being known not just for your achievements but for your character.

Throughout my journey, I've learned that leadership is not about control; it's about empowering others. Whether you're leading a small team or a large organization, your ability to inspire, uplift, and support those around you will define your legacy. Take time to invest in your team's growth, encourage their ideas, and acknowledge their contributions. A thriving business is built not by one person but by a collective effort guided by a shared vision.

Your Next Steps

As you move forward, remember that the entrepreneurial journey never truly ends. Each chapter brings new challenges and new opportunities. Stay curious, stay resilient, and stay passionate about your dreams. There will be times when you feel like giving up, but those are the moments when you must dig deep, find your strength, and keep pushing forward.

Surround yourself with mentors, peers, and supporters who believe in your vision. Seek advice when you're unsure, and offer your own wisdom when others need guidance. Community and collaboration are vital—don't isolate yourself in times of struggle. Sharing your story and learning from others will enrich your journey and help you overcome challenges more effectively.

You have within you the potential to create, innovate, and make a difference. Trust that your efforts will yield results, even when the outcomes are not immediately visible. Stay patient and persistent, and remember that your journey is about progress, not perfection.

As you continue to build and grow your business, keep your passion alive and your purpose clear. Lead with intention, learn from your mistakes, and never lose sight of the bigger picture. You have come this far for a reason—keep pushing, keep dreaming, and keep building.

Your story is still unfolding. Write it with purpose, passion, and perseverance. The world needs your vision, your creativity, and your courage. Keep going—you've got this.

REFLECTION PROMPTS

1. What long-term goals have you set for your business, and how do they align with your vision?

_____

_____

_____

_____

_____

2. How do you balance short-term successes with your long-term strategic vision?

_____

_____

_____

_____

_____

3. In what ways can your business model become more sustainable and community-focused?

_____

_____

_____

_____

_____

Mindset Check-In

"Am I building a business that will stand the test of time? How can I ensure that my success is both sustainable and impactful?"

Prayer

Lord, guide me as I plan for the future of my business. Help me to build with wisdom and integrity, focusing not just on profit but on lasting impact. Give me the strength to stay true to my vision while adapting to the challenges I may face. Thank you for the opportunities you have given me, and help me to honor them by building a business that serves both my community and Your purpose. Amen.

CONCLUSION:

FINAL WORDS OF ADVICE

You made it to the end of this book, and hopefully, the beginning of a new mindset and a bold chapter in your entrepreneurial journey. If there's one truth I've learned along the way, it's this: you don't have to be perfect to be powerful. You just have to be committed. Committed to growth. Committed to healing. Committed to building—even when the blueprint isn't clear.

As you step forward, I want you to remember that your story, your struggle, and your success all matter. You are not alone in this. You are qualified, chosen, and fully capable of creating the business—and the life—you were called to build.

Let this book serve not just as inspiration, but as a reminder: you can rewrite the narrative. You can break the code. And you can leave a legacy worth talking about.

WHAT'S NEXT

This book was just the beginning. I created it to walk with you through the mindset shifts and mechanics of entrepreneurship. But now it's time to move into action. Here's how you can continue the journey:

1. Use the Appendices to start mapping out your business today.
2. Join my online community through The CEO Speaks for coaching, resources, and support.
3. Download bonus materials, planners, and templates at my Stan Store.
4. Follow me on social media for weekly motivation and real-time business tips.
5. Consider booking a strategy session to get personalized feedback and business clarity.

Thank you for trusting me to be a part of your growth. Now go out there and break the code—because the world needs what only you can build.

APPENDICES

APPENDIX A: BUSINESS STARTUP CHECKLIST

☐ Clarify your business idea

☐ Conduct market research

☐ Choose a business name

☐ Secure a domain name and email address

☐ Choose a legal business structure (LLC, S-Corp, etc.)

☐ Register your business with your state

☐ Apply for an EIN (Employer Identification Number)

☐ Open a business bank account

☐ Set up bookkeeping and financial tracking

☐ Create a basic business plan

☐ Outline your products or services

☐ Determine pricing

☐ Create your brand identity (logo, colors, fonts)

☐ Build a website or landing page

☐ Set up social media business accounts

☐ Begin marketing and networking

APPENDIX B: TOOLS FOR ENTREPRENEURS

- Business Structure & Legal
  - ZenBusiness
  - LegalZoom
  - IRS.gov (for EINs)
- Branding & Design
  - Canva
  - Fiverr
  - 99designs
- Websites & Funnels
  - Wix
  - Squarespace
  - Stan Store
  - Shopify
  - ClickFunnels
- Financial Management
  - QuickBooks
  - Wave
  - Google Sheets with automation
- Scheduling & Client Management
  - Calendly
  - HoneyBook
  - Square Appointments
- Marketing & Content Tools
  - ChatGPT
  - CapCut
  - Meta Business Suite
  - Mailchimp / ConvertKit

Appendix C: Sample Business Plan Template (1-Page Format)

Business Name:

_____

Mission Statement:

_____

Target Audience:

_____

Problem You Solve:

_____

Your Solution:

_____

Marketing Strategy:

_____

Revenue Model:

_____

Startup Costs & Pricing Strategy:

_____

Growth Plan (6–12 months):

_____

APPENDIX D: SCRIPTURES FOR ENTREPRENEURS

- Jeremiah 29:11 – God's plans for you are for good and not for harm.
- Proverbs 16:3 – Commit your work to the Lord, and your plans will succeed.
- Habakkuk 2:2 – Write the vision and make it plain.
- Philippians 4:13 – You can do all things through Christ.
- Deuteronomy 8:18 – God gives the power to create wealth.
- Psalm 37:4 – Delight in the Lord and He will give you the desires of your heart.

APPENDIX E: ENTREPRENEUR AFFIRMATIONS

- I am qualified to lead and build.
- I am not behind; I'm right on time.
- I attract divine connections and opportunities.
- Every day I grow in clarity, confidence, and consistency.
- My business is a solution to someone's problem.
- I am walking in my purpose boldly and unapologetically.

APPENDIX F: NOTES SECTION

Use this space to reflect, jot down ideas, or begin outlining your business strategy.

_____

_____

_____

_____

_____

_____

_____

_____

_____

_____

_____

_____

APPENDIX G: MARKETING PLAN TEMPLATE

1. Executive Summary:

_____

_____

2. Target Market Description:

_____

_____

3. Unique Selling Proposition (USP):

_____

_____

4. Marketing Goals:

_____

_____

5. Marketing Strategies:
   • Social Media Strategy

_____

_____

   • Email Marketing

_____

_____

• Influencer Collaborations

_____

_____

• Paid Advertising

_____

_____

• Content Marketing

_____

_____

6. Budget Allocation:

_____

_____

7. Metrics for Success (KPIs):

_____

_____

8. Marketing Calendar (90-day launch strategy):

_____

_____

APPENDIX H: INVESTOR PITCH DECK OUTLINE

1. Cover Slide (Company Name, Logo, and Tagline)

2. Problem Statement (What problem are you solving?)

3. Solution Overview (Your product/service and how it solves the problem)

4. Market Opportunity (Market size, trends, and customer demographics)

5. Business Model (How you make money)

6. Traction (Milestones, current sales/users, partnerships)

7. Marketing & Growth Strategy (Customer acquisition plan)

8. Competitive Analysis (Key competitors and your advantage)

9. Financial Projections (Next 3–5 years: revenue, expenses, profit)

10. The Team (Founders, advisors, key players)

11. Ask (How much funding you need and what it will be used for)

12. Closing Slide (Contact info and thank you message)

APPENDIX I: RECOMMENDED BOOKS AND RESOURCES

- Books to Shift Your Mindset and Money Habits
  - Rich Dad Poor Dad by Robert Kiyosaki
  - The Millionaire Next Door by Thomas J. Stanley
  - The Big Leap by Gay Hendricks
  - We Should All Be Millionaires by Rachel Rodgers
  - Atomic Habits by James Clear
- Podcasts for Business & Motivation
  - The Goal Digger Podcast by Jenna Kutcher
  - Online Marketing Made Easy by Amy Porterfield
  - Earn Your Leisure
  - The Mind Your Business Podcast by James Wedmore
- Courses & Online Learning
  - Goldman Sachs 10,000 Small Businesses Program
  - MasterClass – Business and Leadership
  - Coursera – Entrepreneurship Specializations
  - LinkedIn Learning – Small Business Courses
- Entrepreneur Communities
  - Urban League Entrepreneurship Center
  - NAWBO (National Association of Women Business Owners)
  - Black Women's Wall Street
  - Facebook & LinkedIn Groups for Women Entrepreneurs
- Grant & Funding Opportunities
  - Hello Alice – Small Business Grants
  - IFundWomen
  - Amber Grant for Women
  - Local SBA Offices and Community Development Organizations